50 SUPER E-HACKS

ACTIONABLE INSIGHTS FOR BUSINESS BUILDERS

KARL R. LAPAN

authorHOUSE

AuthorHouse™
1663 Liberty Drive
Bloomington, IN 47403
www.authorhouse.com
Phone: 833-262-8899

© 2024 Karl R. LaPan. All rights reserved.

No part of this book may be reproduced, stored in a retrieval system, or transmitted by any means without the written permission of the author.

Published by AuthorHouse 10/26/2024

ISBN: 979-8-8230-3132-5 (sc)
ISBN: 979-8-8230-3131-8 (hc)
ISBN: 979-8-8230-3133-2 (e)

Library of Congress Control Number: 2024916121

Print information available on the last page.

Any people depicted in stock imagery provided by Getty Images are models, and such images are being used for illustrative purposes only. Certain stock imagery © Getty Images.

This book is printed on acid-free paper.

Because of the dynamic nature of the Internet, any web addresses or links contained in this book may have changed since publication and may no longer be valid. The views expressed in this work are solely those of the author and do not necessarily reflect the views of the publisher, and the publisher hereby disclaims any responsibility for them.

INTRODUCTORY THOUGHTS

These 50 Super E-Hacks are a comprehensive business development guide for navigating the complexities and uncertainties of the entrepreneurial journey. E-Hacks delves deep into nuances of the business-building process, offering invaluable insights, strategies, and practical advice to help entrepreneurs through this challenging but enriching journey. Drawing from multiple decades of coaching, mentoring, and consulting with early-stage companies and the collective wisdom from learned lessons, these supercharged "E-Hacks" are designed to empower you and give you confidence on your entrepreneurial journey. Whether you're a novice entrepreneur just starting or a seasoned business owner looking for new perspectives, you will find something of value within these pages.

This book is reimagined from its companion book - **Entrepreneurial Hacks | Practical Insights for Business Builders** - chock full of practical and actionable meta-insights - covering everything from mastering the art of effective leadership and cultivating a winning organizational culture to leveraging the power of marketing and branding to build stickiness and emotional connections with your customers. This curated content goes beyond the basics to explore advanced strategies for achieving sustainable growth and long-term organizational and personal success. Learn how to navigate challenges and lean into your passion with resilience, adaptability, and composure.

To get the most out of this business resource, lean into the self-assessment questions, be reflective, and be intentional about your discovery and learning. Take the time to seek out mentors, trusted advisors, and peers to delve deep into applying the concepts to your big ideas, your product, and your venture.

Discover how to get you and your business to the next rung of success.

Each section is packed with practical tips and real-world examples, making these ideas and the lessons transferable and easy to implement in your day-to-day operations. Whether you're looking to launch a startup, scale your business, or stay ahead of the competition, this is your actionable guide to achieving higher levels of entrepreneurial success.

DEDICATION

This book is dedicated to my incredible and inspirational 96-year-old aunt – Louella Pachalis – a powerful force for good, the most gracious ambassador of hospitality I know, someone who cares for and puts others first and finishes strong in all she does. She is still doing and caring for others every day, and she taught me so many lessons about life, family, and being present for others.

ACKNOWLEDGEMENTS

This book would not have been possible without the guidance, support, editing, and curating of content of the following individuals: Mark Long, Ted, Baker, Sara Dagen, Vikram Patel, Elliott Welker, Jennifer Harrell and Lilly Withers. Design services provided by Blue Llama Design.

AUTHOR'S NOTE

This book is the result of over twenty-four years of guiding, mentoring, coaching, and supporting entrepreneurs and business builders. Their generosity and vulnerability informed my point of view for an action-oriented approach to accelerating the growth and development of high quality, high performance and sustainable ventures.

BOOK PROCEEDS

The proceeds from the sale of this book will benefit the UF Innovate | Accelerate Greater Gator Good Fund for the advancement of entrepreneurial programs, services, and capital support provided by our UF Innovate | Accelerate program to entrepreneurs in North Central Florida.

KARL-ISMS

I have relied on the following core business sayings throughout my professional career. These *"Karl-isms"* have guided my business behaviors, beliefs and managerial judgment process for decades. Some are my philosophical statements, and others are wisdom nuggets I have learned from individuals, advisors, mentors, and bosses far smarter than me.

About Incubators and its Clients:

- "We are in the "scratch and dent" business." (describing incubator clients.)
- "I will not be held hostage by the inmates running the asylum." (entitled individuals damaging community-building.)
- "The Director is the program." (best practices on why some programs are more successful than others and how effective leadership sets the tone for a quality placemaking program.)
- "If you met one entrepreneur, you have met one entrepreneur."
- "Meet people where they are. There will be less disappointment."

About The Customer Experience:

- "ABCD - **A**lways **B**e **C**onnecting the **D**ots"
- "Focus always on reducing friction."
- "Inspect what you expect."
- "It pays to complain."
- "Show ready - Never know who may show up."

Career Life Lessons:

- "You must be present to win."
- "Double down when others are retrenching."
- "Stay in your lane."
- "Speed wins. If it can be done now, do it now. Sense of urgency in all you do."
- "Always have a product you are peddling."
- "Never negotiate with terrorists."
- "Never get on a ladder. Disability only pays 2/3rds."
- "99% of all people and their families are dysfunctional and the other 1% lie about it."
- "You can't take it with you."
- "Cash is king. It's all about cash, cash, cash, and in that order."
- "Live your life in the windshield, not in the rearview mirror."
- "Time is your enemy."

Career Leadership Lessons:

- "Relationships matter. Invest widely and deeply."
- "Warfare not welfare."
- "The world doesn't need more Monday morning quarterbacks."
- "Snipers are everywhere."
- "Stab me in the heart, not the back. I will respect you more."
- "If you don't know your business better than your boss, you are likely not needed."
- "Ownership and accountability are twin sisters."
- "Take no prisoners."
- "No surprises."
- "It is all about showing up. That's half the battle."

Contents

1. Leadership & Organizational Culture 1

    Super Hack 1 | History Favors the Bold 2
    Super Hack 2 | Change with the Times…or Else 7
    Super Hack 3 | Don't Stop Climbing 12
    Super Hack 4 | Unlocking Your Business Potential 16
    Super Hack 5 | Put 'Em Up 20
    Super Hack 6 | The Power of Delegating 25
    Super Hack 7 | Habits of Effective Entrepreneurs 30
    Super Hack 8 | Discovering Your "Why" 34
    Super Hack 9 | Success, Significance, and Legacy 39

2. Innovation & Entrepreneurship 46

    Super Hack 10 | Stepping on the "Innovation Gas" 47
    Super Hack 11 | Lean into the Things You Love 51
    Super Hack 12 | You're More Than the Phone in Your Hand ... 55
    Super Hack 13 | Entrepreneurship is Boundaryless 60
    Super Hack 14 | Adaptive Pivots Can Help You Stay
        Ahead of the Curve 68
    Super Hack 15 | Courage, Failure & Resilience Go Hand
        in Hand 73
    Super Hack 16 | Setbacks and Mistakes Drive Growth
        and Learning 78
    Super Hack 17 | Know What Makes You Special 83
    Super Hack 18 | Consistency Is Key 88
    Super Hack 19 | The Do's of Innovation 92
    Super Hack 20 | The Don'ts of Innovation 96
    Super Hack 21 | Get Your Head in the Game 100
    Super Hack 22 | Cultivate the Entrepreneurial Spirit 105

3. Marketing & Branding 113

    Super Hack 23 | Building Authentic & Engaging Customer
        Relationships 114
    Super Hack 24 | Memorable Moments Keep Customers
        for Life 120
    Super Hack 25 | Know Your Value 128
    Super Hack 26 | Know Who Wants What You Are Selling 134

4. Personal & Business Development 142
   Super Hack 27 | Positive Well-being Makes You & Your Team Healthier 143
   Super Hack 28 | Grit Is an Elixir 149
   Super Hack 29 | Who Wrote the Rule That Funding Has to Come with Giving Up Ownership of Your Company? 155
   Super Hack 30 | Pitch Like a Pro 160
   Super Hack 31 | Be a 'Purple Cow' 165
   Super Hack 32 | Get Yourself Some Money 170
   Super Hack 33 | Redefining Success on Your Terms 175
   Super Hack 34 | Stop and Smell the Roses 180
   Super Hack 35 | Tips for Launching Your Venture 184
   Super Hack 36 | Learn from Their Marketing Mistakes 189
   Super Hack 37 | Growing Pains 194
   Super Hack 38 | Growth Mode 199
   Super Hack 39 | Throw in the Towel 204
   Super Hack 40 | Goal Setting 208
   Super Hack 41 | Switch it Up 212
   Super Hack 42 | The Art of Self-Sabotage 217
   Super Hack 43 | Discovering Your "Why" 221
   Super Hack 44 | The Power of Perseverance 225
   Super Hack 45 | The KonMari Method 229

5. Networking & Relationship Building 240
   Super Hack 46 | Get Stronger Together 241
   Super Hack 47 | All for One and One for All 247
   Super Hack 48 | You Only Get One First Impression 252
   Super Hack 49 | Back to Basics 256
   Epilogue & Final Super Hack 50 | 24 Years of Working with Inspirational Business Builders: 10 actionable insights 261

1. Leadership & Organizational Culture In Brief

Leadership and organizational culture are the elements that allow successful businesses and institutions to grow. Leadership is substantially more than just mere authority. It embodies vision, inspiration, and guidance. It sets the tone for organizational culture – a complex structure of values, beliefs, and behaviors that define how members interact and work together. Effective leadership cultivates a culture of trust, collaboration, and innovation, driving performance and fostering resilience. Conversely, a toxic culture can destroy morale and impede progress. This section examines the interplay between leadership and organizational culture, analyzing their profound influence on employee engagement, decision-making processes, and overall effectiveness.

Super Hack 1 | History Favors the Bold
3 practices company leaders can embrace to manage uncertainty

During the height of the COVID-19 crisis, the challenge of managing uncertainty in business became apparent. Implementing structured rituals and routines to foster stability, allocating time for rejuvenation and strategic action to manage energy levels effectively, and creating an environment conducive to uninhibited creativity and bold thinking emerged as essential strategies.

> **Self-Assessment Questions:**
>
> 1. How effectively do you embrace rituals and disciplined habits in your daily routine to create stability and predictability in your business activities, especially during times of uncertainty?
>
> 2. What strategies do you employ to make space for rejuvenation, reflective thinking, and actions that manage your energy and well-being while juggling the demands of work and life?
>
> 3. Are you actively encouraging and allowing creative and bold thinking in your approach to managing uncertainty in your business, and are you open to unconventional ideas that challenge the status quo?

Super Hack 1 | History Favors the Bold
3 practices company leaders can embrace to manage uncertainty

GE icon Jack Welch once said the time to invest is during economic paralysis and uncertainty when the less daring is waiting on the sidelines.

Well, managing risks and uncertainty in business can be perplexing. During the depths of COVID, I suffered many sleepless nights as I considered worrisome scenarios:

· What if none of our clients would return to our incubator because of stay-in-place orders?

· What if the federal government shut us down for an extended time or

· What if changing entrepreneurial habits and attitudes that caused everyone to work remotely resulted in higher workplace engagement rates?

If we hadn't found creative ways to remain open and keep people safe during the crisis, we might have been one of those nonprofit statistics: half were in danger of closing due to the pandemic. My team and I didn't want to be that statistic.

Even without a worldwide crisis, unpredictability is a constant in business -- which you likely know whether you're a new entrepreneur or a seasoned executive leading a large corporation. What can help you manage those uncertainties?

Let's look at three practices that can help: embracing rituals, making space for rejuvenation and action, and letting ideas flow.

Embrace rituals.

Building disciplined habits is essential for managing uncertainty in business. When you have a routine, you create a sense of stability and predictability in your day-to-day activities.

> Make sure you set aside time each day to do something that brings you joy, such as exercising, reading a book, or spending time with loved ones. These choices will help you avoid living with regret.

I find clarity in my day's pattern, rhythm, and cadence. For example, I schedule my day to maximize my effectiveness and decision-making. This approach might include not scheduling meetings after 4 pm, reading necessary research and studies at a specific time or week, or blocking parts of my day to ensure reflection time to focus my decision-making.

These techniques can help you stay focused and productive, even in chaos. Sticking to a routine can reduce the likelihood of getting distracted by unexpected events and better manage your time, choices, and energy.

Consider such patterns in these famed entrepreneurs. Amazon founder Jeff Bezos doesn't make important decisions after a specific time of day. Apple founder Steve Jobs reduced "decision fatigue" by wearing the same outfit daily.

The critical point is to reduce unimportant choices in your life and focus on the crucial things that matter.

Make space for rejuvenation, reflective thinking, and action.

Work-life balance has always been mythological to me. I look for work-life integration. It is about your energy and less about your time. By managing your energy, you can gain power over your life.

Some things that work for me include taking team walks early or late in the day, connecting and debriefing situations with my leadership team outside the office, meeting and interacting with people at breakfast or lunch, and seeking new knowledge to develop professionally and personally.

Something I have never been good at but now do, thanks to my Oura™ Ring[1] is having a short meditation each night before bed. I also have prioritized healthy sleeping habits – and these changes have positively impacted my well-being.

Daniel Pink, author of *The Power of Regret*,[2] found in his research that people regret the times they failed to be bold ("If only I had taken the chance") and the moments they were unable to connect ("If only I had reached out"). His book centers on past regrets' power to direct future decisions, leadership, and self-development.

By balancing your time between work and life priorities, you can better handle stress and maintain a positive outlook, even when things feel uncertain, and you can better avoid significant regrets.

Let ideas flow.

Uncertainty in business often requires creative and bold thinking. When you allow yourself to dream without restrictions, you can develop novel approaches you might not have considered otherwise. Don't worry about whether your ideas are practical or feasible – just let them flow freely. You can continually refine them later.

Consider restaurateur Danny Meyer,[3] who continually reimagined his restaurants with the provocative statement to challenge the status quo, "**Who wrote the rule?**" For example, who wrote the rule that a restaurant had to have a parking lot? Or who wrote the rule that a sandwich couldn't cost more than $20?

Managing uncertainty in business requires a combination of discipline, intentionality, and creativity. By building disciplined habits, balancing your time between work and relaxation, and letting ideas flow, you can confidently increase your chances of success and navigate uncertain times.

Remember, while uncertainty may be inevitable, how you respond to it is within your control — **speed and confidence matter**. Invest in both.

Super Hack 2 | Change with the Times...or Else
How to foster an empowered culture so your employees and your company thrive

The essence of organizational culture is more than just a buzzword – it's a driving force behind a company's success and appeal. In today's ever-changing business landscape, where startups rise, and established companies reinvent themselves, cultivating an empowered culture is a survival tactic. Change is a necessity. Cultural transformation requires a proactive approach grounded in clear values and behaviors.

> **Self-Assessment Questions:**
>
> 1. How effectively do you involve employees at every level in defining and promoting the desired values and behaviors that contribute to your company's culture?
>
> 2. Regarding aligning your business with your mission, vision, and values, how well do you integrate these cultural principles into business processes like performance management, talent acquisition, and training programs, and link performance metrics and incentives to encourage desired behaviors?
>
> 3. Are you actively measuring the effectiveness of your cultural transformation efforts through metrics like attrition rates, employee engagement, and customer feedback mechanisms? How do you use these insights to refine your approach to building a dynamic and adaptable organizational culture?

Super Hack 2 | Change with the Times...or Else
How to foster an empowered culture so your employees and your company thrive

"Man, I'd like to be part of their team!"

It was a passing comment from a colleague in another department about my staff, who had just completed another round of "surprise and delight" (ice cream treats this time) throughout the building.

It warmed my heart to think we'd created a company culture so attractive that it made others want to be part of it.

But it also underscored the importance of organizational culture, which plays a pivotal role in shaping the success and longevity of any company.

In today's rapidly evolving business landscape and massive swings in how work is done, fostering an empowered culture is essential for organizations to thrive, <u>especially startup companies</u>[4] that attract talent because of their culture ("the soul of a startup").

"The measure of intelligence is the ability to change," Albert Einstein once said.

Define a set of desired values and behaviors.

Cultural change begins with a clear understanding of the values and behaviors that you aspire to cultivate. While leaders must collaborate to define these principles and ensure they align with the company's core purpose, you don't create culture alone.

Promote ownership and commitment to cultural transformation by involving all your employees at every level.

First, communicate your company's desired values and behaviors – not once, but regularly. Company-wide meetings, newsletters, and intranet updates are tools you can use to convey these values and demonstrate their relevance in everyday operations.

But living them is critical. We say, "Be the change you want to see," and it's valid for business culture and our culture. By consistently acting out and reinforcing these principles, you and your leadership team can create a shared sense of purpose and direction among your employees.

At UF Innovate | Accelerate, we all feel called to a higher purpose. It is a privilege to serve our clients who put it all on the line and risk everything to make the world a better place – whether it is racing for a cure to a rare disease, developing software to solve complex crop quality problems, or putting the next imaging system in space.

Align business with mission, vision, and values.

For cultural transformation to be successful, it must permeate all aspects of an organization, including its business strategies, processes, and decision-making. Aligning the business with its mission, vision, and values is essential to maintain consistency and ensure a coherent organizational identity.

You must integrate the desired values and behaviors into the company's fabric by embedding them in crucial business processes, such as performance management, talent acquisition, and training programs.

By aligning these processes with the cultural transformation goals, you can ensure that individuals who embody the desired values are recruited, recognized, rewarded, and developed.

Moreover, cultural alignment can be reinforced by linking performance metrics and incentives to the desired behaviors. When employees see their efforts toward cultural change are acknowledged, rewarded, and reinforced, they become more motivated and engaged in nurturing the desired cultural shift.

Measure the effectiveness of your efforts.

Measuring the effectiveness of cultural transformation efforts is crucial for continuous improvement and accountability. Organizations should establish clear metrics to evaluate progress and identify areas that require further attention.

Ask your employees for feedback. Make sure they know they will be heard if they speak. You can use employee feedback mechanisms, such as surveys and focus groups, to provide valuable insights into the cultural climate and help gauge the alignment of behaviors with the desired values.

> To make a shift in your company culture, you need to realize it is an ongoing process that requires dedication, commitment, and continuous evaluation.

Another way to measure effectiveness is by tracking key performance indicators related to attrition or retention rate (an employee's first year and over time), employee engagement rate, customer feedback mechanisms (<u>Happy or Not Kiosks [or its app], NPS</u>,[5] for example), or behavioral alignment in performance appraisals with self-assessments or team-level feedback.

Measurement can indicate cultural transformation's impact on your business outcomes. Assessing these regularly allows you to adapt your strategies and interventions accordingly. It enables you to celebrate successes, address challenges, and refine your approach to cultural change, thus nurturing a dynamic and adaptable organizational culture.

The Society for Human Resource Management[6] offers some valuable tips; I especially embrace this: "**Be bold and lead.**"

Do you want to attract top talent and cultivate a positive workplace culture in which you empower your employees and drive organizational excellence? Be bold and lead this cultural shift – and communicate how essential it is for your team to embrace and lean into change together.

Culture building is a team sport – the responsibility of everyone in the organization. And to the benefit of everyone in the organization.

A culture so attractive that others also want to be a part of it.

Super Hack 3 | Don't Stop Climbing
Hit a plateau (or worse)? Here's how to move in the right direction

When faced with a slowdown in business growth, it's easy to get discouraged and lose sight of your goals. However, during these challenging times, your ability to pivot and refocus becomes crucial. Exploring effective strategies for moving in the right direction when you hit a plateau or encounter obstacles in your business journey is important. Take actionable steps to reignite momentum and drive your business forward. Embrace difficult moments as opportunities for growth and innovation.

Self-Assessment Questions:

1. How often do you take the time to reflect on your organization's past achievements, milestones, and positive feedback from customers or clients to celebrate successes and gain insights for future growth when faced with challenges?

2. Have you recently reconnected with your initial motivation and core purpose for starting your business? Do you actively use these sources of inspiration to reignite your drive, especially during periods of stagnation?

3. When experiencing a slowdown in business growth, do you regularly analyze your actions and strategies, seeking feedback from employees, mentors, or customers to identify areas for improvement in your approach?

Super Hack 3 | Don't Stop Climbing
Hit a plateau (or worse)? Here's how to move in the right direction

When facing adversity, it's easy to become fixated on failures and obstacles. But dwelling on setbacks only hinders progress. Instead, shift your perspective by focusing on your organization's successes.

Take stock of past achievements, milestones reached, and positive feedback from customers or clients. Celebrating these wins boosts morale and reminds you of your business's potential for success.

Moreover, by reframing your focus on your organization's success, you can identify patterns and strategies that have worked well, providing valuable insights for future growth.

You should not throw failures out of your mind. People grow more from their failures than their successes. The times you struggle the most can be incredible motivators and lessons to learn from in the future.

Emotionally intelligent people use failure to their advantage[7].

Adversity often brings out your personal best and lets the creativity juices flow.

Take a moment to reconnect with your original inspiration. Reflect on what ignited your entrepreneurial journey, the problems you aimed to solve, or the impact you wanted to make. Revisit your core purpose. Reaffirm your "why."[8]

Reconnect with your motivation.

As an entrepreneur, you likely started your business with passion and motivation. However, over time, it's easy to lose touch with these initial feelings, especially during periods of stagnation or setbacks.

By reconnecting with your motivation, you can reignite the fire within you and regain the enthusiasm needed to propel your business forward.

People today value flexibility and freedom, especially regarding work-life integration. A majority of business owners love the idea of having freedom and passion for the work they are doing. They are also fascinated by building something for themselves from the ground up.

For most, these are often even stronger <u>sources of motivation</u> [9] than money. Reflecting on serving entrepreneurs for over 24 years, I have worked with a few business builders who started their companies to make money.

No. What they wanted was more important: each wanted to change the world. Or reduce friction. Or resolve significant customer pain points.

Recharge yourself and take action.

When experiencing a loss of momentum, reflecting on your actions and strategies is crucial. Analyze what may have contributed to the slowdown and identify areas that need improvement. Consider seeking employee, mentor, or customer feedback to gain fresh perspectives.

Use this reflection as an opportunity to pivot or refine your business approach.

Additionally, remember to recharge yourself personally. Prioritize self-care, take breaks, and engage in activities that inspire and rejuvenate you. By investing in your well-being, you'll be better equipped to face challenges head-on and inspire your team with renewed energy.

Experiencing a lull in business growth can be disheartening, but it's important to remember that it's a temporary phase that can be overcome. By reframing your focus on success, reconnecting with your motivation, and reflecting on your actions, you can reignite the momentum of your business.

Embrace these moments as opportunities for growth and innovation. Remember, setbacks are not indicative of failure but often are stepping stones to success.

So, take a deep breath, refocus, and prepare to propel a better version of yourself and your business to new heights.

Super Hack 4 | Unlocking Your Business Potential
Adding your first employee could be the key to faster success

The journey from a solo operation to a thriving enterprise marks a pivotal transition that requires careful consideration and strategic planning. As a solo entrepreneur, the allure of freedom and self-determination may have propelled you forward, but as your business flourishes, the need to expand beyond solitary endeavors becomes apparent. Explore the critical milestone of hiring your first employee. This decision is not taken lightly, as it involves weighing cultural, financial, and business implications. Discover how to navigate the path toward growth and success, one strategic decision at a time.

Self-Assessment Questions:

1. Have you assessed your financial preparedness for transitioning from a solo entrepreneur to a thriving enterprise by ensuring you have a reserve fund to handle unexpected emergencies and seize unforeseen opportunities?

2. Are you open to reassessing and refining your business model to adapt to changing market trends, meet evolving customer needs, and position your business for sustained growth?

3. Do you maintain your passion for your business while channeling it into disciplined planning, such as creating a strategic roadmap, developing efficient processes and systems, and inspiring your team with the same enthusiasm and commitment that initially fueled your entrepreneurial journey?

Super Hack 4 | Unlocking Your Business Potential
Adding your first employee could be the key to faster success

Being the Chief Everything Office (CEO) has its benefits and drawbacks—isolation and loneliness.

If "it's lonely at the top" of success, it's lonelier at the top of something as new and unproven as a startup. Entrepreneurs often need a team to thrive.

But transitioning to a +1 status – the critical milestone of hiring your first employee – shouldn't be a flippant decision.

It's essential to consider the cultural, financial, and business implications of a +1 before making this decision. Understanding the business case (skill augmentation, time constraints, growing book of business) clarifies the timing of this strategic decision.

Being a solo entrepreneur can be an exhilarating journey filled with freedom and self-determination. However, as your business starts to flourish, you reach a point when you need to expand beyond the confines of a one-person operation.

The first hire can be tricky and risky. The founder of Smart Passive Income [10] Pat Flynn, started his entrepreneurial journey by paying contractors to get work done while he was a one-person operation. However, a time came when he needed more people around who could help him grow, so he made his first hire, his virtual assistant.

"The experience blew me away—it was like I'd been able to clone myself and get twice as much done," Flynn said. "There was no way I'd ever return to trying to do it all myself."

Maybe you're considering your +1 or more, knowing it's time for expansion. Now is the time to make significant changes to reach your business's potential. In today's hack, I'll tell you how.

Save some money.

Establishing a reserve fund is one of the first steps in transitioning from a solo entrepreneur to a thriving enterprise.

You should have at least <u>six months of operating expenses in savings</u> [11] This fund serves two critical purposes: handling unexpected emergencies and capitalizing on unforeseen opportunities.

Emergencies, such as equipment failure or economic downturns, can have a detrimental impact on your business. By building a reserve fund, you create a financial safety net to weather such storms and ensure the continuity of your operations.

A reserve fund lets you seize opportunities to propel your business forward, such as investing in new technologies, expanding your team, or pursuing strategic partnerships.

Reassess, refine, and pivot as needed.

You may have built your business around your unique skills and strengths as a solo entrepreneur. However, to scale and grow, it is essential to reassess and refine your business model.

Take a step back, analyze your market, and identify areas for improvement or expansion. Consider diversifying your products or services, targeting new customer segments, or exploring alternative distribution channels.

This process of reiteration and pivoting allows you to adapt to changing market trends, meet evolving customer needs, and position your business for sustained growth. Embrace the idea that your business model is not set in stone but can grow with time and new opportunities.

Stay passionate in your practice.

Passion [12] is often the driving force behind successful entrepreneurs, and harnessing that passion is crucial for growth. As you transition from a solo entrepreneur to a team-based operation, channeling your passion into disciplined planning becomes even more vital.

Infuse your discipline and planning with the passion that initially ignited your entrepreneurial journey. This combination will empower you to navigate challenges, inspire your team, and maintain the momentum needed for substantial growth.

> Create a strategic roadmap that outlines your goals, timelines, and actionable steps. Develop processes and systems to streamline operations, delegate responsibilities, and foster collaboration among your team members.

Transitioning from a solo entrepreneur to a thriving business with a team is an exciting yet challenging endeavor. You can unlock the true potential of your enterprise.

Remember, growth requires embracing change, taking calculated risks, and staying committed to continuous improvement. As you embark on this transformative journey, embrace the opportunities and nurture your entrepreneurial spirit.

Dare to grow beyond the lonely solo entrepreneur mindset. Move beyond Chief Everything Officer to Chief Executive Officer – casting the vision and strategy to a teammate who helps you do everything better and faster.

Super Hack 5 | Put 'Em Up
Embrace healthy competition to fuel your passion

Competition is everywhere in the fast-paced business world, drawing inspiration from the iconic scene of the Cowardly Lion in The Wizard of Oz. Like the Lion, organizations and entrepreneurs often face formidable opponents in their quest for success. However, rather than cowering in fear, this hack encourages embracing competition as a catalyst for growth, innovation, and excellence.

Self-Assessment Questions:

1. How well do you embrace competition as a driving force for growth and innovation in your business? Are you viewing competitors as motivators, pushing you to improve your offerings and stay relevant in the market consistently?

2. In conducting a competitor analysis, how thoroughly do you understand the strengths, weaknesses, and market position of your competitors? Are you learning from their successes and mistakes to fine-tune your business strategy?

3. Internally, how effectively do you foster a healthy competitive environment within your organization? Are you encouraging healthy Interactlons among team members, settIng clear performance metrlcs, and rewarding outstanding achievements to drive excellence?

Super Hack 5 | Put 'Em Up
Embrace healthy competition to fuel your passion.

You might recall the Cowardly Lion in The Wizard of Oz when the Scarecrow and the Tin Man snuck up on him. He opined,

"Put 'em up, put 'em up! Which one of you first? I'll fight you both together if you want. I'll fight you with one paw tied behind my back. I'll fight you standing on one foot."

Competition applies to the King of the Forest and all of us in the fast-paced business world. Facing competition is inevitable for organizations and entrepreneurs. No matter how groundbreaking or unique your idea, <u>direct or indirect competitors</u>[13] will constantly be vying for the same market share.

McDonald's, Wendy's, and Burger King are perfect examples. Each fast-food chain is slightly different in how it approaches its business model, its customers, its proprietary business processes, its hiring and employee selection, and how it differentiates itself.

Rather than fearing this trait of the business landscape, embrace competition to drive growth, innovation, and success. Competitive strategy is about *being different* and *not just better* than your competitors.

Competitors are everywhere.

No matter how revolutionary your product or service may be, rest assured that someone else is thinking along the same lines. This makes a comprehensive environmental assessment or <u>competitor analysis</u>[14] vital.

More than that, entrepreneurs should understand that competition is an inherent part of the business ecosystem. Instead of viewing competitors as threats, consider them as motivators. They compel you to stay on your toes, consistently improve your offerings, and remain relevant in an ever-changing market.

When it comes to smart money, they know a startup can seldom create a new market from scratch. I often hear founders proudly say, "I have no competitors."; "My product is unique, and no one in the world is like me." For savvy investors, this is a red flag. It is unlikely that any startup has the "fuel" to establish a new market from scratch fully.

Thankfully, having competitors indicates demand for what you are offering. It validates the viability of your business idea and can even provide opportunities for collaboration or partnership within the industry.

The key lies in acknowledging the competition, respecting their presence, and channeling your energy into differentiating and distinguishing yourself in the market. Finding inspiration, not imitating your competitors, is critical to long-term success.

Learn from them.

Competitors can offer invaluable lessons and insights that will help you refine your business strategy. Conduct thorough research to understand their strengths, weaknesses, and position in the market. Analyze their customer feedback, marketing tactics, and pricing strategies.

Learning from their successes and missteps enables you to identify gaps in the market and fine-tune your value proposition. Always look for what makes you different, unique, and memorable. As a mentor of mine once told me, "Look to others for inspiration, not comparison." This timeless advice would serve each of us in business and life.

However, while learning from competitors is critical, avoid falling into the trap of imitation. Instead, focus on what sets your business apart.

Whether it's superior customer service, innovative features, or a more sustainable approach, finding your niche will allow you to attract a loyal customer base, even in the face of competition.

Aspire Higher.

Competition isn't confined to the external market alone; it can also be fostered internally within your organization. Encouraging healthy interactions among team members[15] can drive individual and collective excellence.

> Highlight your unique selling points and leverage them to create a distinct identity in the minds of consumers.

When employees are part of a high-expectations and excellence culture, it can fuel creativity, boost productivity, and nurture continuous skill development and self-improvement. These skills equip employees with intellectual curiosity, drive, and resilience for the challenging day's entrepreneurial journey.

Set clear performance metrics and reward outstanding achievements to foster a positive competitive environment. Encourage teamwork while recognizing and celebrating individual efforts. Implement training and development programs that enable employees to build on their strengths and acquire new skills, making them better equipped to face challenges.

Moreover, avoid fostering a toxic atmosphere where employees prioritize personal gain over the organization's success. Emphasize the importance of collaboration, support, and shared goals. Healthy competition should act as a catalyst for growth rather than a divisive element within the team's dynamic.

Overall, competition in business is not to be feared but embraced. Recognizing competitors is a natural part of the landscape and can provide valuable insights on what to do differently. By adopting this mindset, you can position yourself to thrive in a dynamic and competitive business world.

Super Hack 6 | The Power of Delegating
3 tips for gaining control of your load
while scaling your company

Delegation is a fundamental skill for leaders and entrepreneurs seeking sustainable success. Effective delegation majorly impacts productivity, growth, and employee empowerment. By analyzing your schedule, outsourcing menial tasks, and regularly checking in with employees, you can lighten your load, focus on more critical activities, and foster collaboration and accountability within your organization.

Self-Assessment Questions:

1. How effectively do you control your schedule to identify tasks that could be delegated, allowing you to focus on more important activities? Are you prone to handling everything yourself, or are you mindful of potential burnout and inefficiency?

2. To what extent do you recognize the value of your time as a leader and entrepreneur? Are you open to hiring or outsourcing tasks that are routlne, menial, or outside your expertise? How well do you prioritize strategic decision-making and important activities over mundane tasks?

3. How actively do you continuously communicate and collaborate with your team members after delegating tasks? Do you view delegation as a one-time transaction or prioritize regular check-ins to discuss progress and challenges?

Super Hack 6 | The Power of Delegating
3 tips for gaining control of your load while scaling your company

Effective delegation [16] has emerged as a crucial skill for leaders and entrepreneurs in every industry. It's easy to feel like you should be fully involved in everything your company does, but it's impossible.

Delegating tasks lightens your load, empowers teams, enhances productivity, and fuels growth.

The trick is knowing what to delegate and how to keep the results of tasks you've delegated at the same level of excellence (always strive for perfection but settle for excellence) – or better than – you'd expect from yourself. Here's how:

Analyze & take control of your schedule.

As leaders, it is easy to fall into the trap of wanting to handle everything ourselves, but this can lead to burnout, lost productivity, and inefficiency.

You can start the delegation process by thoroughly analyzing your daily, weekly, and monthly activities to show areas where your time, expertise, and energy could be used better.

Recognizing inconsistencies in your schedule and determining which tasks can be offloaded is essential for effective delegation and greater employee empowerment.

Outsource menial tasks.

As you complete that analysis, recognize the value of hiring or outsourcing menial and routine tasks – or simply those outside your scope of expertise. (Yes, someone might do something better or differently than you. That's a good thing!)

As a leader, you must realize that your time is valuable and should be dedicated to strategic decision-making and high-impact activities.

Entrusting mundane or repetitive tasks – or those requiring specialty skills -- to competent individuals allows you to focus on critical aspects of your business that need your expertise.

What is it that only you can do? Time is energy, so you must decide where to place your effort for the highest impact.

Whether administrative duties, data entry, marketing, or social media management, <u>outsourcing such tasks to qualified professionals</u> [17] can significantly streamline your workflow. By delegating these responsibilities, you not only free up time but also benefit from the expertise of specialists in those areas, leading to better results.

Moreover, hiring external experts can bring fresh perspectives and innovative ideas, contributing to overall organizational growth.

Check-in with employees.

Delegation should not be a one-time transaction; it necessitates continuous communication and collaboration. You'll find many benefits arise from <u>delegation in leadership</u>.[18]

Regularly checking in with employees to discuss delegated tasks can improve workflow and productivity. Encouraging an open dialogue allows team members to share their thoughts on the assigned tasks, providing insights into potential challenges or areas that could be optimized.

Employees who feel their opinions and ideas are valued become more invested in the delegated tasks. This sense of ownership drives them to perform better and contribute actively to the team's success.

Additionally, discussing progress and roadblocks fosters a culture of transparency and accountability, ensuring that tasks are on track and aligned with the organization's objectives.

Delegating responsibilities ensures you have the right person in the proper role (if you hire well!), builds morale while sharing your company's vision, and freeing you to drive the company to be its best.

Final Thoughts

Think about successful people like Amazon's Jeff Bezos, who only makes decisions during certain core hours when operating at peak performance. Or a successful executive who intentionally prioritizes the rhythm of life components – physical, emotional, intellectual, and spiritual to achieve a higher level of well-being.

Tasks that do not align with your core competencies or strategic priorities are strong candidates for delegation. Offload such responsibilities to capable team members or outsourcing partners. You'll ease your burden and empower others within your organization, fostering growth and development.

> Attention to detail is a hallmark of uber-successful companies that achieve consistent, high-impact results. Companies that reach that hallmark have leaders who delegate, inspire, and collaborate with their team members.

Mastering the art of delegation is crucial for any leader or entrepreneur looking to achieve sustainable success. Embracing delegation as a strategic tool enables leaders to foster a more agile, productive, and successful business environment while upskilling key team members.

Super Hack 7 | Habits of Effective Entrepreneurs
Follow your dreams and make these three a habit

Foundational business practices set successful business builders apart and drive them towards their goals. While some individuals may possess innate talents, the majority can compensate by developing the habits of highly effective entrepreneurs. Dreaming big, starting small, and scaling fast are stepping stones to more robust visionary thinking, allowing them to innovate and navigate challenges smoothly.

Self-Assessment Questions:

1. How effectively do you think with a mindset of dreaming big and envisioning a future beyond the status quo? Do you challenge conventional thinking and explore different possibilities and outcomes for your business?

2. How well do you prioritize your physical and mental well-being while navigating the entrepreneurial journey? Do you recognize the importance of self-care in maintaining productivity and creativity?

3. How effectively do you manage your time and prioritize tasks to maximize productivity and success? Are you proactive in setting clear goals and establishing a structured schedule that aligns with your business objectives?

Super Hack 7 | Habits of Effective Entrepreneurs
Follow your dreams and make these three a habit

Gallup's widely used Builder Profile 10 identified that 2.5% of the population has the rare and special talent to be top-notch business builders. What if you're an entrepreneur who aspires to the top-notch level, but you're not part of that elite percentage?

You could make up for it by developing the *habits* of effective entrepreneurs. They're driven by unique habits that set them apart, shape their business strategies, and influence their personal lives.

Successful entrepreneurs consistently embrace these practices to achieve their goals. It's important to dream big, but having effective habits that allow you to reach your goals systematically is just as important.

Consider Walt Disney [19] He was fired from his newspaper job for not being creative enough – but we all know that's false. Disney had dreams big enough to drive him to build the entertainment empire many have come to love. He used his passion to inspire new ideas and, intent on succeeding, found ways to turn them into reality.

You, too, will succeed if you follow your dreams with passion and intent. It's the first of three habits setting apart effective entrepreneurs.

Dream big, Start Small, Scale Fast.

Vision is the cornerstone of every successful entrepreneurial journey. Effective entrepreneurs dare to dream big [20] and envision a future others may not see. They think outside the box, challenge the status quo, and ask, "What if?"

For instance, consider the story of a tech entrepreneur who envisioned a world where people could connect instantly, irrespective of distance. This visionary thinking gave birth to a social media giant that transformed our ways of communicating today.

By dreaming big and continually questioning the potential of their ideas, effective entrepreneurs can turn dreams into reality and leave a lasting impact on the world.

Take care of yourself.

The entrepreneurial journey can be exhilarating but comes with its fair share of stress and challenges. Effective entrepreneurs understand the importance of self-care [21] and prioritize their physical and mental well-being.

Burnout is a real threat in entrepreneurship's high-pressure world; neglecting self-care can hinder productivity and creativity.

> By exploring different possibilities and outcomes, they can anticipate challenges and seize opportunities others might miss. This habit enables them to innovate and remain agile in an ever-changing business landscape.

Successful entrepreneurs make time for activities that rejuvenate their minds and bodies, such as regular exercise, meditation, spending time with loved ones, or pursuing hobbies and outside interests.

By caring for themselves, they can maintain the energy and focus necessary to tackle obstacles and stay resilient in adversity.

Spend your time wisely.

Time is a finite resource, and effective entrepreneurs know its value. They recognize that how they spend their time directly impacts their productivity and overall success. Time management is not just about being busy but rather about being intentional and purposeful with every minute.

Entrepreneurs who succeed in managing their time prioritize tasks based on their importance and urgency. They set clear goals and establish a well-structured schedule that allows them to focus on high-impact activities while delegating or eliminating non-essential ones.

This habit ensures they achieve their business objectives and allows them to strike a balance between work and personal life. Paying attention to one's energy and directing it toward things with the most significant impact separates highly effective entrepreneurs from run-of-the-mill business builders.

Effective entrepreneurs possess a unique set of habits that propel them toward success. Whether your talents land you in the elite 2.5% of naturally gifted business builders or not, embracing these habits can foster success in business and lead to a more fulfilling and purpose-driven entrepreneurial journey.

So, if you aspire to be an effective entrepreneur, start cultivating these habits and witness the transformative power they unleash. Remember, on average, it takes 66 days of consistent effort for a new behavior to become a habit!

Super Hack 8 | Discovering Your "Why"
3 ways to be an authentic company

From cultivating a strong identity to inspiring trust and motivation, to embodying ethical leadership that permeates throughout the organization, examine how your vision and values influence every facet of business operations. Consider the significance of fostering innovation by integrating it into the core values, empowering employees to contribute ideas, and fostering a culture of continuous improvement.

> **Self-Assessment Questions:**
>
> 1. How effectively does your company embody its stated vision and values, both externally in branding and internally in operations? How does consistency in adhering to these ideals build trust?
>
> 2. Are the leaders in your organization demonstrating ethical behavior that aligns with the company's values? How does ethical leadership set the tone for the entire organization, fostering a positive work environment where trust and collaboration thrive?
>
> 3. How does your company encourage a culture of innovation that aligns with its vision and values? How do you empower employees to suggest new ideas and approaches, ensuring your company stays ahead of the competition?

Super Hack 8 | Discovering Your "Why"
3 ways to be an authentic company

In the dynamic and ever-evolving business world, having a clear vision and a set of solid values is paramount. These pillars define a company's identity and serve as a compass for navigating the turbulent seas of commerce.

Let's delve into three crucial aspects of harnessing the power of vision and values in business.

Strong identity

A company's identity can be its most potent weapon in a marketplace flooded with choices. Your vision and values should be the foundation of your brand. It's not enough merely to articulate these ideals; you must embody them consistently.

> Consistency in branding builds trust. Customers notice when you consistently adhere to your stated vision and values – and they feel a sense of security interacting with you.

They become your identity. When they encounter such a company, they know what to expect, and this predictability can foster loyalty.

This also applies to internal operations. When your employees see that your company aligns with its words, they are likely to embrace your purpose and take pride in their work. This commitment can lead to increased motivation and productivity.

Positive behavior

Ethical leadership[22] is a must in today's business landscape. Harvard Business Review reporters Nicholas Epley and Amit

Kumar discuss "How to Design an Ethical Organization" in a 2019 magazine article.

In it, they point to Wells Fargo's deceptive sales practices between 2002 and 2016, which resulted in a $3 billion penalty,[23] and Uber's failure to disclose a massive data breach, which cost the company a $148 million settlement.[24]

In addition to the financial costs of such behavior, Epley and Kumar say, "Unethical behavior takes a significant toll on organizations by damaging reputations, harming employee morale, and increasing regulatory costs."

The actual behavior of its leaders – much more than any marketing material – must reflect a company's values. The adage "Actions speak louder than words" certainly rings true here.

Ethical leadership sets the tone for the entire organization. When leaders are transparent, honest, and fair, employees are more likely to trust their guidance. Trust, in turn, fosters a positive work environment in which collaboration and innovation thrive.

I remember a headhunter who called me for an incredible job opportunity. It was to do strategic planning for a company with smoking products. I declined because I didn't want to be responsible for providing strategies that led people to be more addicted to nicotine.

He told me he would never call me again, and he didn't. But I have never looked back on that moment with regret. I had watched my father (who smoked since he was 14) die of lung cancer. I didn't want anyone else to suffer such a loss.

Social injustice, environmental concerns, and other problems also influence your customers. Today, consumers demand more socially responsible companies [25]

They want the brand they support to address social and environmental issues, and many of those consumers pay close attention to those efforts when making purchase decisions.

Drive for innovation

Innovation [26] is the lifeblood of a successful business. Your vision and values should be constant but evolve with the times. Encourage a culture of innovation by weaving it into your core values.

Employees should feel empowered to suggest new ideas and approaches that align with the company's vision. When innovation becomes part of your identity, you are better equipped to adapt to changing market conditions and stay ahead of the competition.

Remember, innovation doesn't always have to be groundbreaking; it can be about continuous improvement. Encourage small, incremental changes that add up to significant advancements over time.

The relentless pursuit of innovation excellence is no accident. The most successful companies have a performance culture that cultivates the implementation of innovation as a consistent business discipline.

A company's vision and values are more than words on a page or a sign hanging on your wall; they drive your success. By being firm and consistent about your company's identity, leading ethically, reinforcing positive employee behavior, and always being open to innovation, you can build a resilient and thriving business, no matter the ever-changing business landscape.

Embrace these principles – these pillars of vision and values – and your business will stand firm in the face of challenges and continue to grow and prosper.

Super Hack 9 | Success, Significance, and Legacy
3 stages of a fulfilled and blessed life

Success encompasses not only financial achievements but also personal and professional goals, positively impacting society, and fostering a thriving work environment. Building significance involves making a meaningful impact through social responsibility, sustainability, and ethical practices, inspiring others with values that transcend profit. Creating a legacy takes the concept of significance further, focusing on making a lasting mark, nurturing organizational culture, and leaving an impact that endures through generations.

Self-Assessment Questions:

1. How do you prioritize personal and professional goals alongside financial gains? How can you ensure that your pursuit of success positively impacts both your stakeholders and society as a whole?

2. How do you currently contribute to social responsibility, sustainability, and ethical practices within your organization?

3. What steps are you currently taking to ensure the continuity of your business's values, vision, and impact for future generations? How can you invest in leadership development, mentorship programs, and succession planning to leave a lasting imprint beyond your tenure as a leader?

Super Hack 9 | Success, Significance, and Legacy
3 stages of a fulfilled and blessed life

As a business professional, the pursuit of success often takes center stage. However, many entrepreneurs and leaders recognize there's more to business than just the bottom line. Exploring the concepts of success, significance, and legacy in business is essential, each with its unique value and impact. Recently, I talked to one of my sons about legacy and how you can't just skip over the steps or sidestep life's pain and create a short path to your legacy. We don't just wake up leaving a legacy. We accumulate one every day through our actions and our choices. It is not single-event driven. My mentor and close friend had an index card behind his desk with the three words – Success > Significance > Legacy. He reminded me that he was deeply invested in impact, being present, and growing his relevance even after hitting 80+ years old.

Chasing success

Business success is often synonymous with profitability, growth, and market dominance. While these are undeniably important, pursuing success should encompass more than just financial gains. True success in business means achieving personal and professional goals, positively impacting society and others (paying it forward), and fostering a thriving and energizing work environment. We all seek belongingness and meaningful connections. We want to add value and have others see value in us.

Successful businesses set clear objectives, implement efficient strategies, and adapt to changing market dynamics. They also prioritize the well-being of their employees, fostering a culture of collaboration, innovation, and work-life balance. Success is not merely about the destination; it's about the journey and the positive influence a company can have on its stakeholders.

Building significance

Significance [27] in business goes beyond success. It's about making a meaningful and lasting impact on the world. A significant business stands for more than profit; it stands for purpose. A deep commitment to social responsibility, sustainability, and ethical practices drives businesses that chase significance.

To build one's significance (relevance), businesses and individuals often engage in philanthropy, support societal and charitable causes, and prioritize economic and social prosperity and opportunity. They understand that their actions can shape not only their industry but also society at large. A significant business inspires employees, customers, and partners by exemplifying values that transcend the balance sheet.

Leaning into legacy

For entrepreneurial ventures, Legacy [28] in business takes the concept of significance a step further. It's about creating a lasting imprint beyond the founder's tenure. A legacy-driven business seeks to build a foundation for future generations, ensuring the continuity of its values, vision, and impact. Successful entrepreneurs often turn to venture philanthropy, civic leadership or establish a donor-advised fund, family office, or foundation. Businesses that lean into legacy usually invest heavily in leadership development, mentorship programs, and succession planning. They understand that building a legacy requires a strong, enduring organizational culture that can thrive without constant supervision. Such companies leave a mark not only through their products or services but also by nurturing the potential of their people.

For individuals leaning into legacy, there is often a restlessness, anxiety, and an urgency around leaving your mark or thinking about how you might be remembered. This is where you usually reflect on your biggest regrets, missed shots on goals, or do-overs.

Pursuing success, significance, and legacy in business represents a continuum of ambition and purpose. As business leaders, it's crucial to balance these three dimensions, recognizing that they are not mutually exclusive.

> One of the best pieces of advice I have received is to "live your life in the windshield, not in the rearview mirror." Thinking back, it is probably a much healthier place to be.

While success is essential for survival and growth, significance elevates a business's role in society, and legacy ensures its impact endures through generations.

End Notes for Leadership & Organizational Culture

1. "Oura Ring: Accurate Health Information Accessible to Everyone," Oura Ring, accessed September 22, 2023, https://ouraring.com.
2. Daniel H. Pink, *The Power of Regret: How Looking Backward Moves Us Forward* (New York: Riverhead Books, 2022).
3. Ann Graham, "Danny Meyer's Recipe for Success," Strategy+business, accessed September 22, 2023, https://www.strategy-business.com/article/Danny-Meyers-Recipe-for-Success.
4. Ranjay Gulati, "The Soul of a Start-Up," *Harvard Business Review*, July 1, 2019, https://hbr.org/2019/07/the-soul-of-a-start-up.
5. "Performance Indexes," accessed September 25, 2023, https://support.happy-or-not.com/s/article/Performance-indexes.
6. Christina Folz, "10 Tips for Changing Your Company's Culture—and Making It Stick," SHRM, June 27, 2016, https://www.shrm.org/resourcesandtools/hr-topics/employee-relations/pages/10-tips-for-changing-your-companys-culture—and-making-it-stick.aspx.
7. Travis Bradberry, "8 Ways Smart People Use Failure To Their Advantage," Forbes, accessed September 25, 2023, https://www.forbes.com/sites/travisbradberry/2016/04/12/8-ways-smart-people-use-failure- to-their-advantage/.
8. *Start With "Why" - TED Talk from Simon Sinek*, 2016, https://www.youtube.com/watch?v=2Ss78LfY3nE.
9. "The No. 1 Reason Most Entrepreneurs Start Businesses - Businessnewsdaily.Com," Business News Daily, accessed September 25, 2023, https://www.businessnewsdaily.com/4652-entrepreneur-motivation-benefits.html.
10. Pat Flynn, "20 Entrepreneurs Reveal Their First Hire Story: How & When They Grew Their Team," Smart Passive Income, April 1, 2019, https://www.smartpassiveincome.com/blog/20-entrepreneurs-reveal-their-first-hire-story/.
11. "How Much Should You Have in Business Savings | Treasure," accessed October 16, 2023, https://www.treasurefi.com/blog/how-much-should-you-have-in-business-savings.
12. Clate Mask, "Passion, Freedom and Impact: The 3 Ingredients of Business Success," Entrepreneur, January 31, 2015, https://www.entrepreneur.com/leadership/passion-freedom-and-impact-the-3-ingredients-o f-business/240396.
13. "Direct vs. Indirect Competition, Explained," accessed January 12, 2024, https://blog.hubspot.com/marketing/direct-indirect-competition.

14. "What Is a Competitive Analysis — and How Do You Conduct One?," October 11, 2022, https://blog.hubspot.com/marketing/competitive-analysis-kit.
15. Expert Panel, "Council Post: Eight Ways To Foster Healthy Competition Among Your Team Members," Forbes, accessed January 12, 2024, https://www.forbes.com/sites/theyec/2022/07/27/eight-ways-to-foster-healthy-competition- among-your-team-members/.
16. Expert Panel®, "Council Post: 14 Delegation Strategies That Will Help Entrepreneurs Build A Business," Forbes, accessed January 26, 2024, https://www.forbes.com/sites/forbescoachescouncil/2020/11/17/14-delegation-strategies-t hat-will-help-entrepreneurs-build-a-business/.
17. "(30) 10 Daily Tasks That You Should Be Delegating So You Can Focus On Growing Your Business | LinkedIn," accessed January 26, 2024, https://www.linkedin.com/pulse/10-daily-tasks-you-should-delegating-so--1e/.
18. "Delegation in Leadership: Do's and Don'ts," accessed January 26, 2024, https://www.indeed.com/.
19. "Walter Elias Disney," Entrepreneur, October 8, 2008, https://www.entrepreneur.com/growing-a-business/walter-elias-disney/197528.
20. Jodie Cook, "8 Reasons You Should Be Dreaming Bigger," Forbes, accessed February 7, 2024, https://www.forbes.com/sites/jodiecook/2020/06/01/dream-bigger/.
21. Deep Patel, "8 Self-Care Tips From Wildly Successful Entrepreneurs," Entrepreneur, February 4, 2019, https://www.entrepreneur.com/living/8-self-care-tips-from-wildly-successful-entrepreneurs/326643.
22. Nicholas Epley and Amit Kumar, "How to Design an Ethical Organization," *Harvard Business Review*, May 1, 2019, https://hbr.org/2019/05/how-to-design-an-ethical-organization.
23. "Office of Public Affairs | Wells Fargo Agrees to Pay $3 Billion to Resolve Criminal and Civil Investigations into Sales Practices Involving the Opening of Millions of Accounts without Customer Authorization | United States Department of Justice," February 21, 2020, https://www.justice.gov/opa/pr/wells-fargo-agrees-pay-3-billion-resolve-criminal-and-civil-in vestigations-sales-practices.
24. "Uber and the Ongoing Battle Over Consumer Data Privacy," Bloom Blog, September 28, 2018, https://bloom.co/blog/uber-and-the-ongoing-battle-over-consumer-data-privacy/.
25. YEC, "Council Post: How Corporate Responsibility Is Influencing Consumer Buying Decisions," Forbes, accessed April 8, 2024, https://www.forbes.com/sites/theyec/2022/05/02/how-corporate-responsibility-is-influencin g-consumer-buying-decisions/.

26 Young Entrepreneur Council, "Council Post: 12 Smart Ways To Encourage Employee Innovation," Forbes, accessed April 8, 2024, https://www.forbes.com/sites/theyec/2019/05/02/12-smart-ways-to-encourage-employee-i nnovation/.
27 Jonathan Knowles et al., "What Is the Purpose of Your Purpose?," *Harvard Business Review*, March 1, 2022, https://hbr.org/2022/03/what-is-the-purpose-of-your-purpose.
28 Glenn Llopis, "What Legacy Would You Leave Behind If You Left Your Company Today?," Forbes, accessed April 26, 2024, https://www.forbes.com/sites/glennllopis/2017/09/23/what-legacy-would-you-leave-behind-if-you-left-your-company-today/.

2. Innovation & Entrepreneurship In Brief

Innovation and entrepreneurship are the critical forces driving businesses forward, reshaping industries, and revolutionizing operations worldwide. From groundbreaking technological advancements to disruptive business models, these concepts represent the catalyst for progress in the modern world. With creativity, risk-taking, and strategic vision, innovation sparks new ideas and transforms them into tangible solutions. Entrepreneurship embodies the bold pursuit of these ideas, navigating challenges and seizing opportunities to bring them to fruition. This section explores how innovation and entrepreneurship bolster businesses by fostering adaptation, driving growth, and recognizing competitive advantage in ever-changing markets.

Super Hack 10 | Stepping on the "Innovation Gas"
Elevate your innovation journey with insights from Entrepreneurial Hacks

Dive headfirst into the world of innovation. Recent headlines have spotlighted larger companies' dilemmas, where economic uncertainties and short-term thinking have cast shadows over their innovation investments and cultural priorities. This prompts us to revisit innovation fundamentals and explore how organizations can cultivate a culture that fosters creativity, embraces risk-taking, and thrives on collaboration.

> **Self-Assessment Questions:**
>
> 1. How effectively does your organization encourage and support you and your colleagues in taking risks and trying new ideas, even if they might not have an immediate financial payoff?
>
> 2. To what extent does your company foster a culture of innovation from the top down, where leaders actively participate in innovation initiatives and embed innovation into the company's DNA?
>
> 3. Are there clear processes and transparent communication within your organization regarding how new ideas are evaluated and measured for success and how long they spend in the innovation funnel?

Super Hack 10 | Stepping on the "Innovation Gas"
Elevate your innovation journey with insights from Entrepreneurial Hacks

Recent news reporting sparked a Super Hack. The story suggested that significant tech giants' innovation investments and culture suffer today due to uncertain and mixed economic results, axing large groups of employees and contributing to poor morale and lower employee engagement.

Case in point: Amazon insiders [1] wondered whether the company would prioritize big ideas if they didn't have an immediate financial payoff – rattling key cultural priorities – "thinking big" and "inventing and simplifying."

Several years ago, a Forbes article[2] posited, "At a time of rising uncertainty, an ability to innovate rapidly has never been more important." So, what causes innovative giants to succumb to myopic, short-term thinking at a time when they should be stepping on the "innovation gas"?

Let's relook at some enduring innovation fundamentals.

Innovation is a crucial dimension of success for any organization. Adapting to change, embracing new ideas, and taking risks is essential in today's rapidly evolving business environment. However, creating a culture of innovation in the workplace can be a challenging task. It requires a concerted effort from leaders and employees alike to foster an environment that nurtures creativity, builds organizational confidence, and hones the opportunity-spotting skill set.

This work emphasizes the need for organizations to cultivate a culture of innovation from the top down. This mandate means leaders must be willing to make bets (think Google's significant loss-leading business segment, Other Bets) and encourage their employees to do the same. It also means embedding innovation into the company's DNA in good and bad times. I am often surprised that most organizations must learn what projects are in their innovation funnel. Employees need to know how ideas are judged to survive (and possibly thrive) in the funnel, how long ideas have been in the funnel, and why there are no active conversations in organizations about how the success and viability of new ideas will be measured or chosen for implementation.

One of the critical factors in fostering an innovative culture is **creating an environment that allows for experimentation and failure**. Employees must feel empowered to try new things, even if they might not work out. This "bias for action" requires a certain level of risk tolerance and leaders to provide tools and support to fully actualize a more innovative culture. This "active dialog" creates a culture where failure is reframed as a learning opportunity rather than a cause for blame or punishment.

Another critical aspect of an innovative culture is **collaboration**. Collaboration is often an overused word. For nonprofit organizations, there need to be intentional negotiations around who gets the cash, the credit (for potential success), and the control (whose mission trumps the other partners). There needs to be coherence with the mission and core purpose of the collaborating organizations. Just because they are nonprofit organizations doesn't mean collaboration is a good thing; the only thing they may have in common is that they are both nonprofits!

Encourage employees to hone and build their skills while learning how to connect the dots.

It's important to emphasize the need for organizations to

break down silos and encourage cross-functional teams to work together. This transdisciplinary approach helps foster creativity and new ideas but also helps build a sense of community within the organization. Employees who feel part of a team working towards a common goal are likely to be engaged and invested in their work.

It is also necessary for leaders to be **intentional about creating and spotting opportunities for innovation**. Opportunity spotting means setting aside protected time and resources for employees to work on new projects and explore new ideas (think Post It Notes™).

Innovation is often born out of crisis or opportunity. So, organizations need to be willing to *adapt and cannibalize themselves*. This mindset means being open to new business models, technologies, and working methods that may challenge the status quo or what made that organization successful in the past. It requires a certain level of leadership courage and patient investment, both in good and bad times.

Super Hack 11 | Lean into the Things You Love
3 tips for building resilience so a better you can overcome adversity

With continual challenges and uncertainties, resilience empowers us to bounce back stronger and embrace change with courage and determination. Through insightful reflections and practical advice, we'll uncover the importance of surrounding ourselves with supportive individuals who elevate us, intentionally pursuing personal development, and embracing reinvention as a pathway to self-discovery.

Self-Assessment Questions:

1. Are the people you surround yourself with in your personal and professional life supportive and inspiring, challenging you to become a better version of yourself, and do they help fuel your resilience in overcoming obstacles?

2. How intentional are you about personal growth and self-improvement? Have you identified specific areas for improvement and set clear, actionable goals? Are you cultivating habits aligned with your objectives and consistently prioritizing growth-related activities in your schedule?

3. Are you open to reinventing yourself, embracing change, and pursuing new passions and career paths as opportunities for personal development? How do you view setbacks and failures in your journey toward personal growth as stepping stones to a better future?

Super Hack 11 | Lean into the Things You Love
3 tips for building resilience so a better you can overcome adversity

Life can be challenging, and we sometimes face setbacks, obstacles, and moments of self-doubt. At those times, we need resilience to grow and improve. Resilience empowers us to overcome adversity, bounce back stronger, and embrace the process of reinvigorating ourselves. Keep in mind the following as you lean into the things you love.

Surround yourself with people who make you better.

You might have heard the self-made observation, "You are the average of the five people you spend the most time with." Jim Rohn further said, "If you aren't intentional about the people you spend your time with, you won't be able to gain the continuous personal improvement you seek in life."

The company we keep plays a significant role in shaping our thoughts, beliefs, and actions. When striving for personal growth, we must surround ourselves with individuals who inspire us to become better versions of ourselves. These people are supportive and challenge us to step out of our comfort zones. They also reflect areas where we need to catch up or fall short. Whether they are mentors, friends, or family members, they possess the power to bring out our personal best.

If we're leading companies, we must surround ourselves with smart, trusted advisors. Engaging with such individuals exposes us to new perspectives, ideas, and experiences. They push us to set higher goals and hold us accountable to achieve them. These relationships fuel our resilience and reinvigorate our drive to overcome obstacles.

Remember, success is rarely a solo journey; the right people can aid our path to higher self-actualization.

Be intentional in becoming a better version of yourself.

Growth requires deliberate effort to become the best version of oneself. It begins with honest self-reflection and a deep understanding of our strengths, improvement areas, and aspirations. Take time to identify improvement areas and set clear, actionable goals.

At the same time, double your effort and lean into the things you love. Embrace a growth mindset, acknowledging challenges as opportunities for growth and learning. Being intentional also involves developing habits in line with your growth objectives. Cultivate a routine to make it a habit. Despite myths, a new behavior takes an average of 66 days (or as little as 18 to as much as 254 days) to become automatic and habitual. Today, reflect and consider a habit you'd like to develop. Choose one and build it with discipline, rigor, and repetition. Be intentional.

One way I stay intentional about personal growth is to cast a wide net on the type of meetings I attend. I intentionally cultivate business relationships. I visit business owners (to see patterns and connect dots) to fuel my intellectual curiosity. I am a vociferous and agile learner looking for insights and to connect disparate dots.

Don't have time for such things? Embrace Stephen Covey's object lesson [3] about prioritizing. He suggests you fit the big "rocks" into your calendar first – and then add the more minor stuff. By doing so, you will find time for growth activities and become more effective and valuable to your organization.

Choose reinvention for personal change & self-care.

Our aspirations, passions, and circumstances may evolve as we grow, calling for personal transformation. Embrace the inevitability of change as an opportunity for personal development. I'm sad when people say they don't want to learn things or are comfortable with the status quo. Don't be that person. Reinvent your possibilities. Reimagine your relevance.

Trying new things and taking risks demand courage and willingness. Rise to the occasion. *And if you fail?* Embrace failure as a stepping stone toward success and learn from setbacks. By choosing reinvention, you empower yourself to adapt, grow, and unlock your full potential.

> Step out of your comfort zone. Pursue new career paths. Explore different passions.

Educational futurists predict future generations will have 11-17 careers in a lifetime. This prediction makes me jealous. I might be lucky to have 2-3 careers in my lifetime. We must reinvent our skill sets and be resilient to work in a world where most future jobs have yet to be invented.

Resilience is the key to reinvigorating ourselves and embracing personal growth. Remember, resilience is not just about bouncing back; it's also about leaning forward and using challenges as stepping stones toward a better and brighter future.

So, embrace change, harness your inner strength, and embark on a journey of reinvigoration and personal growth. By doing so, you may just beat your best five-person average!

Super Hack 12 | You're More Than the Phone in Your Hand
What makes you human is what AI and technology can never steal

With growing concerns regarding artificial intelligence disrupting the job market, we're confronted with the profound question of what makes us human and how technology fits into that equation. While technology has become an integral part of our daily lives, its assimilation into the workplace has raised concerns about its impact on genuine human connections and relationships. Technology can enhance but only partially replace the value of authentic human interactions.

> **Self-Assessment Questions:**
>
> 1. In the era of increasing AI and technology influence, how well do you prioritize genuine human interaction in both your personal and professional life, recognizing the value it brings to solving complex issues and fostering quality relationships?
>
> 2. Regarding coordination and collaboration in your work, do you acknowledge the irreplaceable power of face-to-face interactions in building trust, enhancing teamwork, and critical thinking alongside the technological tools at your disposal?
>
> 3. Reflecting on your social and professional connections, how do you balance the convenience of virtual relationships and the value of genuine human Interactions?

Super Hack 12 | You're More Than the Phone in Your Hand
What makes you human is what AI and technology can never steal

The headlines are real. "AI's Threat to Jobs Prompts Question of Who Protects Workers," [4] The New York Times wrote just last week after Sam Altman, CEO of the startup OpenAI, urged a Senate subcommittee to regulate the AI industry – before it was too late.

Goldman Sachs [5] estimated that generative AI -- capable of generating text, images, or other media in response to prompts -- could replace the equivalent of 300 million full-time jobs globally. At the same time, U.S. General Surgeon Vivek Murthy [6] declared loneliness – one of the side effects of technology – a public health threat.

Technology has run rampant – whether it's AI usurping jobs or social media platforms making us feel more alone. Yet, it is also an integral part of our lives in today's digital age. We rely on technology for various aspects of our daily routine, from smartphones to social media to smart refrigerators and cars.

While technology undoubtedly offers convenience and efficiency, it should not be seen as a substitute for quality relationships and human interactions. Some of our well-being issues today can be traced to a lack of human interaction and investment in personal and deep relationships.

Hence, we feel isolated and alone, often on an emotional roller coaster in which the following text, Instagram post, or phone call defines our mood.

Using technology and AI in practically every industry has many benefits, but despite threats, I do not think it can replace every job for even a second. It is also not a panacea for America's "quiet quitting" revolt.

Some roles, let's say sales, for example, cannot be replaced by machines – at least not entirely. As the Harvard Business Review[7] says, "Generative AI will enrich — not erase — jobs."

I hope this is true, but with large corporations disbanding their AI ethics teams, plenty of room for abuse abounds, and the degree of erasure depends.

That's where the hack is – and the AI job threat and technology-propagated loneliness come together. Because some jobs – and all relationships – need the human element, AI and technology can't mimic.

Consider customer solutions.

Technology has undoubtedly revolutionized customer service and support, making it more accessible and efficient. However, nothing can replace the value of genuine human interaction when solving complex issues or providing personalized assistance.

While chatbots and automated systems can handle routine inquiries, customers often seek the empathy and understanding only humans can provide. If customers lose their package in transit, they feel frustrated and seek answers. Having an empathetic, understanding person help them solve their predicament will give them a much better experience.

What about coordination and collaboration?

Technology enables us to collaborate and coordinate with individuals globally effortlessly in today's interconnected world. Tools like video conferencing, project management software, and instant messaging platforms have transformed our work.

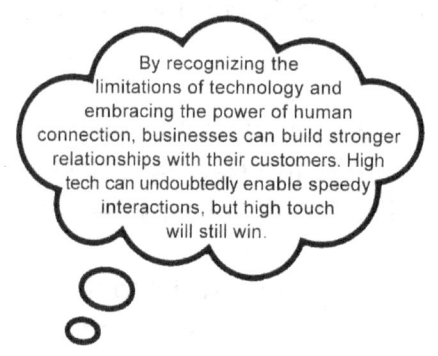

> By recognizing the limitations of technology and embracing the power of human connection, businesses can build stronger relationships with their customers. High tech can undoubtedly enable speedy interactions, but high touch will still win.

However, despite these technological advancements, more is needed to replace the power of face-to-face interactions when fostering trust, enhancing teamwork, and problem-solving on a project.

While technology facilitates coordination and collaboration, Forbes [8] points out, "Humans have the power of critical thinking, which engineers have been unable to reproduce in robots and other technology to date."

Connections are for electronics, but connectivity is for us.

An NCBI article [9] states, "If new automation technologies are unlikely to replace us soon, they will alter how we work."

Social media and online networking platforms have undeniably expanded our social and professional circles, allowing businesses to be successful worldwide. However, the quality of these connections often pales compared to the depth and richness of real-life relationships.

Online interactions lack the spontaneity and intimacy that come with face-to-face encounters. Physical presence facilitates genuine emotional connections, shared experiences, and the ability to understand and empathize with one another honestly.

It is essential to balance the convenience of virtual relationships and the irreplaceable value of genuine human interactions.

I hope these reminders give you hope – and a path forward in a world of technology and AI.

While technology has undoubtedly transformed the way we live, work, and connect, it should not be a substitute for quality relationships and human interactions.

Whether providing customer solutions, fostering collaboration, or building social connections, technology can enhance and augment these experiences but only partially replace the value of genuine human relationships. If we placed more importance on relationships and being present, some of the profound loneliness, despair, and isolation we feel might dissipate, and we could live happier and healthier lives.

By striking this balance, we can create a world where technology empowers us to build stronger connections while preserving the essence of what it truly means to be human.

Being human is something a robot or generative AI can never fully replicate.

Super Hack 13 | Entrepreneurship is Boundaryless
3 things to remember if you want to expand your business & mindset

As we navigate the dynamic landscape of entrepreneurship, we encounter moments of inspiration, setbacks, and triumphs that shape our perspective and drive our ambitions. From fostering a nurturing environment for our entrepreneurial community to embracing the universal lessons of success and failure, keep an open mind to new ideas and professional connections is essential.

Self-Assessment Questions:

1. As an aspiring entrepreneur, do you actively seek innovative ideas from diverse sources, embracing that great ideas can come from any part of the world or even your mind?

2. Are you willing to accept failure as a universal part of the entrepreneurial journey and use it as a stepping stone for growth rather than letting it deter you from taking intelligent risks?

3. Do you recognize the importance of building connections and networks with like-minded individuals, industry experts, mentors, and potential collaborators, understanding that meaningful relationships and support networks can accelerate your entrepreneurial success regardless of geographic boundaries?

Super Hack 13 | Entrepreneurship is Boundaryless
3 things to remember if you want to expand your business & mindset

"The #The HubSweetHome thing is legit," my assistant director said recently.

She was juggling – as usual – multiple balls: a client blowing up her email because they needed access to a mentor, an international client she was connecting to other CEOs in the building, and an inspiring visionary and game-changing group looking for the best and next practices in business incubation from across the state she was sending a follow-up email.

It was not a day in the life of an incubator leader. It was an hour. But rather than overwhelm or frustration, I read the smile.

I share it, too.

We work with special people. Entrepreneurs. They have a vision for something no one else can see – and they put everything they have into making it happen, even when the people they love the most don't understand. Our goal is to reduce or eliminate friction experienced by our clients daily.

It can be a lonely – scary – place. They're misunderstood, told they're crazy to their face, and must often fail to succeed.

So, we try to provide a #HubSweetHome in our facility, The Hub (and a similar vibe in our flagship biotech center, Sid Martin Biotech). However, the entrepreneurs do the heavy lifting for each other. (We are the place makers orchestrating resources, tools, and community for a thriving and aspiring entrepreneurial community.)

Their fellow entrepreneurs get the struggle.

Entrepreneurship transcends borders and cultures, and aspiring entrepreneurs worldwide can learn valuable lessons -- often from each other -- to guide their journey. Individuals from across the globe develop innovative ideas that turn into successful businesses.

Some even take their growth a step further through globalization. [10]

Regardless of how far you decide to expand your business, it's important to remember three key components all entrepreneurs should lean into on their journey.

#1: Great ideas come from all corners of the world

Entrepreneurship knows no geographical boundaries [11] and innovative ideas can originate from unexpected places. (Yes, even your own brain.)

The interconnectedness of our world enables the rapid exchange of ideas, allowing groundbreaking solutions to emerge from diverse perspectives and cultural backgrounds. Entrepreneurs harness their unique insights and connect disparate dots to create disruptive products and services in a remote village or a bustling metropolis. This diversity enriches the entrepreneurial ecosystem, fostering an inclusive and vibrant innovation environment.

Plenty of brilliant minds think up unique, exceptional ideas that make life better, more accessible, simpler, and faster.

Consider the rental umbrella service in Tokyo, Japan [12] The weather in any place can be spontaneous; how many times have you watched the Weather Channel, and everything they said turned out to be just flat wrong?

The "iKasa" service devised an innovative solution for unpreparedness for a sudden downpour. You find one of their umbrella rental locations on your phone, scan a QR code to pick it up, and then scan again when you drop it off at another location closer to your destination—a simple yet effective solution for a common problem.

No doubt Florida weather could benefit from it, given our unpredictable weather.

#2: Failure is universal

Failure is inevitable in the entrepreneurial journey, but don't let that deter you from taking intelligent risks.

Regardless of their location, entrepreneurs face similar challenges and setbacks. However, the key lies in embracing failure as a valuable learning opportunity.

Resilience and the ability to bounce back from failure distinguish successful entrepreneurs. By reframing failure as a stepping-stone to success, you can refine your strategy, pivot (or change course) when necessary, and build a more reliable business model.

"There's a silly notion that failure's not an option at NASA," Elon Musk said. "Failure is an option here. If things are not failing, you are not innovating enough."

Of course, neither NASA nor SpaceX wants to fail when their rockets are loaded with people and flying toward Mars. Fail early and often – well before then – seems a better choice.

Failure should not obstruct intelligent risk-taking but propel entrepreneurs confidently toward their goals. Unfortunately, a global fear of failure remains a top deterrence for aspirational entrepreneurs to move their entrepreneurial interests to action.

#3: Connections matter everywhere

That's where networking can play a vital role.

Building a solid network opens doors to valuable connections, resources, and opportunities. Entrepreneurs must actively engage with like-minded individuals, industry experts, mentors, and potential investors to expand their reach and gain insights.

Like-minded individuals are often other entrepreneurs – not necessarily ones in your field. In our incubation program at UF Innovate | Accelerate, we hold roundtable meetings with a wide variety of industry company C-suite leaders – and while they can choose their vulnerability comfort level, they share struggles and solutions and leave feeling validated, supported, and stronger.

(And sometimes, through these interactions, they are surprised to see how they might collaborate to create a new business angle the world needs now.) Emotional intelligent entrepreneurs see opportunities in connecting disparate dots. They lean into it and look for it in their intentional interactions.

Nurturing meaningful relationships and fostering a supportive network accelerates growth and maximizes your chances of success.

Success often requires doubling your investment in your connections. Gallup studied [13] 4,000 entrepreneurs in 3 different countries, including the United States, and discovered that successful entrepreneurs have a rare set of 10 talents in common.

"Highly successful entrepreneurs -- 2.5% of the population – have the rare and special talent" and can account for all ten talents to build a super-successful business," the Gallup research revealed.

The rest of us need to "account" for all ten talents to grow successful businesses. That means working with others who might have the talents we don't have.

Every community has an ecosystem. How you interact with it and use the assets, resources, and leverage connections can make a difference.

You can find entrepreneurial energy across communities in universities and community colleges, with service providers, resource partners, incubators, coworking sites, accelerators, banking and other capital sources, government agencies/entities, and social service sector players.

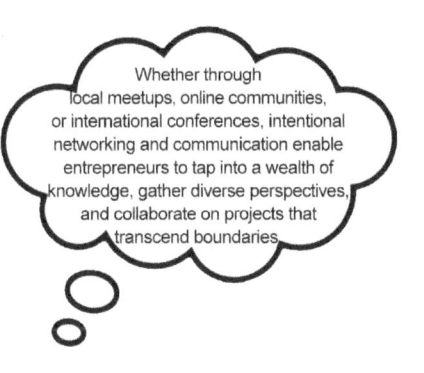

> Whether through local meetups, online communities, or international conferences, intentional networking and communication enable entrepreneurs to tap into a wealth of knowledge, gather diverse perspectives, and collaborate on projects that transcend boundaries.

It truly takes a village to raise a vibrant entrepreneurial community.

This is what I mean.

A case in point is the airport operations industry, which had to rebuild itself globally following the COVID-19 pandemic. After being unable to travel for so long, people were eager to fly.

However, resuming regular operations, implementing new safety standards, and adapting to a rapid increase in customer demand required international communication and collaboration. Not only did air travel return to its pre-pandemic numbers, but as of 2023, the industry's revenue has grown by 16.2%.

How did it manage to succeed? Connections! Connections between entrepreneurs working together to meet travel demands (as well as making sure passengers made their connecting flights...). Global partnerships to make the world more easily accessible. Further, airlines like Delta reported [14] "surges in demand across leisure, corporate, and international markets." Rising demand has placed significant pressure on the operational side of airlines. Indeed, this will result in a wave of new technological innovations and, unfortunately, more regulatory intervention and oversight.

Motivated by opportunity.

Entrepreneurs pay it forward by collaborating with other like-minded people. We see this every day in our UF incubators. When we measured this ecosystem effect, we found that nearly 30% of our companies worked with other companies in our building – with people they did not know before joining our program.

Entrepreneurship is a universal language that inspires individuals worldwide. Great ideas can emerge from any part of the world, leading to success (often through failure). By embracing these universal lessons (and each other), aspiring entrepreneurs can confidently navigate the challenges of entrepreneurship, fostering a global entrepreneurial energy driven by innovation, resilience, and collaboration.

And, if they're lucky enough to connect with the right people, creating their own

#HubSweetHome. Similarly, you cannot help but leave our facilities encouraged and inspired by game-changing science to advance promising medical and biotech breakthroughs.

It is legit and reinforces our "why" every day.

Super Hack 14 | Adaptive Pivots Can Help You Stay Ahead of the Curve
Don't let the hard times keep you down...stay resilient

The ability to pivot strategically is crucial for long-term success and sustainability. Businesses encounter obstacles such as dry spells, market shifts, and regulatory burdens that demand innovative solutions and flexible approaches. Anticipate when and how your business can pivot strategically to effectively overcome challenges and drive growth.

Self-Assessment Questions:

1. As a business leader, do you actively assess your employees' skills and resources during decreased demand or dry spells, seeking opportunities to reassign them to different roles, reallocate resources, or explore new adjacent market opportunities?

2. Are you committed to monitoring market trends and conducting thorough environmental scanning to identify emerging market changes and adapt your business strategies accordingly and quickly, including embracing technology advancements and digital transformation?

3. Have you considered shifting from relying solely on freelancers and temporary help to hiring full-time workers as your business expands and leveraging a mix of full-time and freelance workers for specialized expertise and access to diverse skills?

Super Hack 14 | Adaptive Pivots Can Help You Stay Ahead of the Curve
Don't let the hard times keep you down...stay resilient

When the going gets tough, tough businesses get going – in a different direction if needed.

One of our resident clients made such a pivot when the FDA regulatory burden became so onerous that its product intended for the sanitization and disinfection industry might have failed. The company has found success by switching to the extreme odor elimination market, where it could sell consumer products.

Adapting and making strategic pivots is essential for long-term success in today's ever-changing business landscape. Businesses often face challenges such as dry spells, economic uncertainties, and market corrections that necessitate a shift in strategies and operations.

Let's explore three key areas where businesses can pivot to navigate obstacles and growth effectively to stay ahead of the curve.

Dodge the dry spells.

Businesses often have underused employees and resources during a dry spell or decreased demand. *Remember the Great Recession*[15] *in 2008?* Instead of letting these valuable assets go to waste, a strategic pivot involves reassigning employees to different roles, reallocating resources to maximize "shots on goal," and exploring new adjacent market opportunities.

Additionally, reallocating resources to innovative projects or exploring new market opportunities adjacent to your core business can help diversify revenue streams and mitigate the effects of a dry spell.

For entrepreneurial ventures, I always recommend that "resources should lag opportunity." Cash is still king, and getting too far in front of your business opportunities can substantially reduce your burn rate runway. Consider my five tips for startups during uncertain economic times.

> Shifting employees into different roles allows you to tap into their diverse skill sets and knowledge. You can help your workforce acquire new competencies and adapt to new responsibilities by providing training and development programs.

Adjust to market changes.

Market changes [16] are a constant reality in the business world. Companies that are agile and quick to respond to these changes are better equipped to thrive. A strategic pivot involves carefully monitoring market trends and adjusting your business strategies accordingly.

Conducting thorough environmental scanning is crucial to adjust to market changes. These insights can help you identify emerging trends and adapt your products or services to meet evolving or shifting customer needs.

Additionally, embracing technology advancements and investing in digital transformation can give your business a competitive edge in an ever-evolving market. Your business can retain and grow customer loyalty by focusing simultaneously on efficiency and quality customer experiences.

Robust strategic planning should always involve a comprehensive PEST analysis [17] – thoughtfully considering political, economic, socio-cultural, and technological factors likely to influence and inform a cohesive business's strategy.

This environmental scanning might include evaluating increases in interest rates, assessing geopolitical factors such as the prolonged war in Ukraine, or considering the impact of a recession.

Doing so allows you to spot opportunities, assess, mitigate risks, and adapt to market inflections.

Use contingent workers for access to diverse skills and flexibility.

As your business expands and evolves, it becomes increasingly important to shift from relying on freelancers and temporary help to hiring full-time workers. This strategic pivot allows you to cultivate a dedicated team of employees, foster more vital internal collaboration, and unlock the full potential of your growing business.

In many of today's business models, having a mix [18] of full-time and freelance workers can be beneficial. It allows you to have specialized work done by experts worldwide. Sometimes, after completing a project together, a freelancer with a unique skill set might be a conduit for future talent acquisition.

Today, businesses can compete for open talent[19] by recruiting flexible remote workers with diverse skill sets anywhere globally. Everyone is a "free agent."

Strategic pivots are vital for sustainability and growth in the dynamic business landscape. By embracing change and fostering an adaptable and growth mindset, businesses can position themselves to thrive in an ever-evolving marketplace.

Successful pivots require proactive planning, constant evaluation, and a willingness to embrace new possibilities. It may mean abandoning what has always worked for a new direction.

Which might include extreme odors. Be tough.

Super Hack 15 | Courage, Failure & Resilience Go Hand in Hand
Don't miss this lesson in disguise

From the moment we take our first steps as infants, we begin a lifelong journey of trial and error, learning, and growth. Yet, somewhere along the way, many of us develop a fear of failure that stifles our willingness to take risks and innovate. We should challenge this fear and celebrate failure as a powerful personal and professional development catalyst. Explore the importance of embracing failure as an opportunity for growth and the necessity of testing new ideas despite uncertain outcomes.

> **Self-Assessment Questions:**
>
> 1. Do you embrace failure as an opportunity for growth, understanding that it is a valuable teacher that can propel you forward personally and professionally, and are you committed to analyzing failures to identify areas for improvement?
>
> 2. Are you willing to test new ideas and take calculated risks in your entrepreneurial endeavors, recognizing that experimentation and iterative processes can provide invaluable insights, refine your strategies, and increase your likelihood of future success, even in the face of uncertainty?
>
> 3. Do you possess the courage to face failure, have the resilience to bounce back from setbacks, adapt to change, and continue pursuing ambitious goals despite this fear of failure?

Super Hack 15 | Courage, Failure & Resilience Go Hand in Hand
Don't miss this lesson in disguise

You weren't born with a fear of failure. No. You were born a problem solver who tried, failed, and kept trying.

As a baby, you likely learned to roll over, crawl, and walk – by trying to roll over (and failing) a few times. Once you mastered rolling onto your stomach, you may have gotten on your hands and knees and rocked back and forth, trying to figure out how to reach something you wanted.

You didn't see your parents crawl, but you created that means of transportation alone. You followed it by standing, then taking a step – and falling, getting back up, and trying again. Sometimes it hurts.

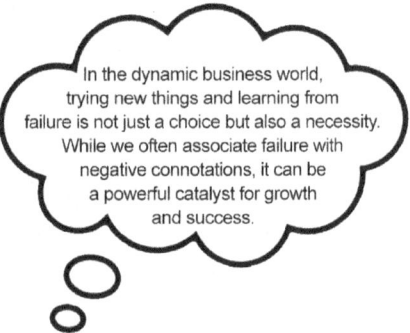

> In the dynamic business world, trying new things and learning from failure is not just a choice but also a necessity. While we often associate failure with negative connotations, it can be a powerful catalyst for growth and success.

But learning from your failures was in you. Fear of failure wasn't.

You need to grasp that strength once again as an entrepreneur.

Let's delve into the importance of using failure as an opportunity for growth, the value of testing new ideas despite uncertain outcomes, and the courage required to embrace and recover from failure.

Failure is an opportunity for growth.

Failure is not a bad word. Innovation only happens with failure. We seldom have the impetus to improve something if someone else got it right the first time. And our attempts aren't often perfect straight off either.

But when entrepreneurs adopt a growth mindset, failures become valuable lessons that propel them forward. Business owners can grow personally and professionally by analyzing what went wrong and identifying areas for improvement.

Failure offers an opportunity to reassess strategies, refine approaches, and acquire new skills. Learning from failure helps avoid the same mistakes and nurtures resilience and adaptability, enabling entrepreneurs to thrive in adversity.

Milton Hershey [20] started the chocolate company we have all come to know and love. However, he started – and failed – three candy companies before finding success with Hershey's chocolate.

It took him four tries – four businesses – to get it right. But he had learned from his previous failures and setbacks – and refused to quit.

Too many people have a fear of failure. That fear is a critical stumbling block, especially among the younger generations.

More than 40% of millennials, who became the largest group in the labor force in 2016, have a paralyzing fear of failure. In addition, studies show that 43% of possible U.S. entrepreneurs [21] are deterred from starting a business due to a fear of failure.

Try new things.

Yet, innovation lies at the heart of successful businesses, and experimentation is the fuel that drives it.

Testing new ideas, even if they don't yield the desired results, can provide invaluable insights and opportunities for improvement. Each failed attempt offers a chance to gather data, evaluate customer feedback, and refine strategies.

This iterative process allows businesses to fine-tune their products, services, and marketing approaches and hone their dynamic business model, increasing the likelihood of future success.

Entrepreneurs who embrace the uncertainty of testing new ideas demonstrate a willingness to take risks, adapt to change, and stay ahead of the competition. Without these brave souls, who knows what we'd be missing?

Baby carrots, for one thing.

Many people don't know this, but baby carrots don't grow on trees – or come out of the ground looking like they do.

A brilliant farmer named Mike Yurosek [22] hated the idea that misshapen or odd-looking carrots got wasted. This was a significant portion of the carrots he would harvest (and Endo Pharma hadn't appeared on the scene to feature bent carrots in its commercials promoting treatment for Peyronie's Disease). [23]

So rather than waste them, Yurosek used a potato peeler to make smaller, better-shaped carrots and keep these imperfect ones from the waste bin. But this process was too long and laborious to mass-produce "baby" carrots.

He refused to quit, however. Instead, he repurposed an industrial green bean cutter to cut carrots into uniform 2-inch pieces. Ta-da! The baby carrot industry was born.

Yurosek tried something innovative – and iterated until he found a solution. It paid off.

Have the courage to fail and recover.

Failure can be daunting, but it is an inevitable part of the entrepreneurial journey. Successful business leaders understand the importance of having the courage to fail and the resilience to bounce back.

Overcoming the fear of failure [24] is critical to unlocking growth and success. It takes courage to step out of your comfort zone, pursue ambitious goals, and face the possibility of setbacks. By reframing failure as a temporary setback rather than a permanent defeat, entrepreneurs can learn from their mistakes, pivot when necessary, and ultimately achieve their objectives.

"Out of every ten things I try, how many do I have to get right to be judged successful in this job?" I once asked a non-profit board.

The arithmetic mean of the group's responses was 8. This set the stage for the organization's risk tolerance. I pondered the reality of innovation: 3 of 1,000 would be world-class, yet I had achieved 8 out of 10. Undoubtedly, in this case, I could only take minimal risk and adopt only sure things (or incremental changes) until the conditions for failure were relaxed.

Is that where you would want to stay? Taking minimal risk and making only incremental changes?

In the realm of business, trying new things and learning from failure is not only essential but also transformative.

View failure as a valuable teacher, providing insights, refining strategies, and propelling your efforts forward. Doing so is paving a brighter and more likely path to success.

The one you were born to follow.

Super Hack 16 | Setbacks and Mistakes Drive Growth and Learning
3 ways to change your mindset from failure to success

As we delve into the benefits of failure and its role in shaping resilience, creativity, and adaptability, we uncover insights to transform setbacks into opportunities. Uncover the power of turning failure into something positive, staying passionate amidst challenges, and cultivating a proactive problem-solving attitude. Remember, failure is not the end but the beginning of your journey toward success.

Self-Assessment Questions:

1. Do you have the ability to channel negative emotions such as frustration and disappointment into positive action when faced with failure, and are you capable of embracing a growth mindset to see setbacks as opportunities for valuable insight?

2. Are you deeply connected to your passion for your business, able to remind yourself of the positive impact you aspire to make, and surrounded by a supportive network of like-minded individuals?

3. Do you have a proactive problem-solving attitude, able to adapt quickly to changing circumstances, break down challenges into manageable steps, and focus on finding solutions rather than dwelling on every setback?

Super Hack 16 | Setbacks and Mistakes Drive Growth and Learning
3 ways to change your mindset from failure to success

"I have not failed 10,000 times, "Thomas Alva Edison, the inventor of the commercially viable electric light bulb, once said, "I've successfully found 10,000 ways that will not work."

His perspective – that quote – sticks with me. One, because it's true. And two, because that's the attitude it takes to change the world or to cure for a better world, as our UF Innovate|Accelerate mission statement reminds us.

And he did. Edison held over a thousand patents for his inventions, many of which made our world brighter and some of which failed to garner widespread support.

Failure is an inevitable part of the business journey, but it doesn't have to have a tragic ending. Successful entrepreneurs understand that setbacks are growth opportunities. It's all about how you interpret your situation and how you act.

Edison interpreted failure well.

Nobody's perfect; making mistakes is a part of life. What's more, failure has benefits:

1. Failures can make you smarter.

2. Failing means you're likely *leaning into* risks and *learning from* them.

3. Failing provides opportunities for iterative growth and pivots.

Again, it's all about the way you interpret your situation. Let's look at how you can improve your mindset to see failure as a benefit.

Turn it into something positive.

When failure strikes, it's natural to feel a wide range of emotions, such as frustration, disappointment, and even self-doubt. Rather than allowing these emotions to overwhelm you, channel them into something positive.

Use the energy from your emotions to fuel your determination and motivation. Take a step back, reflect on the situation, and identify the lessons learned.

Embrace a growth mindset, focusing on how failures can provide valuable insights and opportunities for improvement.

Additionally, keep in mind not all failures are equal.

The Harvard Business Review[25] discusses three types of mistakes: preventable, complexity-related, and intelligent. Understanding how to handle different setbacks effectively will allow you to soften the blow better, recover from the situation, and grow.

If you haven't read Daniel Pink's book, The Power of Regrets, [26] you should. It is full of insight into what people regret most, and what they would want to do if they did it again.

> Seek support from mentors, peers, or business communities to gain new perspectives and guidance. You can transform setbacks into stepping stones toward success by redirecting negative emotions into positive action.

Pink concluded most regrets often center on the loss of connections in relationships. Perhaps, this is a good time for us all to identify an impaired relationship we want to rebuild intentionally.

Stay passionate.

Passion is the driving force behind every successful entrepreneur.

Think about some successful companies and the reason they exist. For example, Google's mission [27] is to "organize the world's information and make it universally accessible and helpful."

When faced with failure, reconnect with why you started your business in the first place. Remember the excitement and enthusiasm that propelled you forward. Reflect on the impact you aspire to make and the value your product or solution brings to others.

Google's workers, from salespeople to computer programmers, are inspired by the company's mission and passion through the value their work carries. Passion provides the necessary fuel to persevere through challenging times.

Surround yourself with a supportive network of like-minded individuals who share your vision and can reignite your passion. Focusing on your purpose and reminding yourself of the positive impact you can make makes failure a temporary setback rather than an insurmountable obstacle.

Cultivate a proactive problem-solving attitude.

I'm not suggesting you try to fail. Resist the temptation to think failure is free or that there are no consequences to failure. Endless pivots may be chock full of learning but probably don't make investors happy. But do embrace failure as an opportunity to grow stronger and more resilient. Resilience is an essential trait for entrepreneurs navigating the unpredictable path of business.

Develop a mindset that treats failure as a valuable learning experience rather than a reflection of your worth.

But don't wait for failure! Instead, cultivate a proactive problem-solving attitude and adapt quickly to changing circumstances. Break down challenges into manageable steps, focusing on finding solutions rather than dwelling on the setbacks.

Remember, even the most successful entrepreneurs faced numerous failures along their journey. With each setback, you gain valuable insights and build resilience to overcome future obstacles.

Failure is not the end; it's an integral part of the entrepreneurial journey. By channeling emotions into something positive, remembering your passion, and developing resilience, you can transform setbacks into real opportunities for personal and business growth.

Embrace early false starts or failures as stepping stones toward success; each experience brings valuable lessons. As you navigate the challenging business world, remember that the most successful entrepreneurs learn from failure and rise above it with determination, passion, and resilience.

But most importantly, remember you can't change the world or innovate a better future without making some mistakes along the way.

After all, you aren't making mistakes. You're successfully finding ways you won't repeat next time.

Super Hack 17 | Know What Makes You Special
Follow these tips to stand out from the competition

Understand the essence of gaining a competitive advantage in today's dynamic business environment. Drawing inspiration from experienced pros like Procter and Gamble (P&G), we explore how identifying and leveraging what sets your company apart is paramount for success. From understanding the intricacies of competitive advantage to embracing uniqueness and adaptability, you uncover the strategies that propel businesses to the forefront of their industries.

> **Self-Assessment Questions:**
>
> 1. Have you identified and articulated the unique strengths and capabilities that give your business a competitive advantage in the market? How effectively are you communicating these differentiators to your target audience?
>
> 2. How well is your competitive advantage aligned with Warren Buffet's "moat" principle? Is your advantage rare, unique, sticky, and memorable? Additionally, are you actively looking for new opportunities to shift and pursue unique advantages?
>
> 3. Are you constantly evolving and adapting your competitive advantage to meet the changing demands of the market and evolving customer preferences? How effectively are you investing in research and development, embracing technological advancements, fostering innovation, and enhancing the overall customer experience to stay ahead of the curve?

Super Hack 17 | Know What Makes You Special
Follow these tips to stand out from the competition

In today's fast-paced and ever-evolving business landscape, gaining a competitive advantage is vital for long-term success. It enables businesses to differentiate themselves from competitors, capture market share, and pursue sustainable growth.

If you want people to buy from you instead of the competition, you must know and sell what makes you unique and special.

For decades, companies such as Procter and Gamble (P&G)[28] have avoided competition by doing just this. Their competitive advantage lies in their "higher standard of excellence — a standard of irresistible superiority across product, package, brand communication, retail execution, and value."

It's infused into the company's DNA. Their advantage comes not simply from what they *do* but from who they *are*.

Or maybe who they *were*.

The company's aggressive pricing post-COVID – tarnishing the "value" aspect of its standard of excellence – has weakened its brand preference and opened the door to alternative and niche products. As consumers flex their financial muscle, these alternatives have put select P&G products on a decline despite P&G buying up some of these brands. As the consumer's wallet is stretched, so is their willingness to break ranks with the brand.

Knowing what makes your company special isn't enough – if you don't follow these other tips to stand out from the competition.

Understanding competitive advantage.

Competitive advantage [29] refers to the unique strengths and capabilities that allow a business to outperform its market rivals. It encompasses various factors, including superior products or services, cost leadership, innovative technology, efficient processes, strong and durable customer relationships, and intellectual property.

Competitive advantage can be derived from combining these elements or a singular standout feature, but it can't be something basic like "we have great customer service." Instead, think more about what your company has that makes customer service exceptional.

Is it your highly trained representatives who undergo a refined training process that ensures success or a helpful AI assistant on your website that helps customers navigate and understand your product or service? How consistent is your brand experience across the customer touchpoints?

I often default to Warren Buffet's "moat" [30] principle to understand how a business can maintain and grow its competitive edge. This analogy refers to companies with a defined moat, or competitive advantage, that allows them to keep other companies away while seeing higher returns in the long term.

> All competitive advantages erode over time, so looking for new opportunities to shift and pursue unique advantages is critical.

Competitive advantages are rare, unique, sticky, and memorable. Companies only sometimes possess more than one, and having one still doesn't guarantee success.

Be different – rare and special.

Competitive advantage is pivotal in making a business stand out by enabling organizations to differentiate themselves in a saturated market, ensuring they are not merely another face in the crowd.

By identifying and capitalizing on their unique strengths, businesses can create a distinct brand identity and position themselves as industry leaders. This differentiation helps attract customers, enhance brand loyalty, and build a strong reputation.

Businesses must identify and leverage their unique selling points to gain a competitive advantage.

Evolving your competitive advantage – never static.

In addition, you need to be able to adapt. [31] Investing in and evolving your competitive advantage is crucial for long-term success, as a static competitive advantage is unlikely to sustain growth in the face of changing market dynamics and growing customer preferences.

Businesses must continuously assess their competitive landscape, monitor industry trends, and adapt their strategies accordingly. This may involve investing in research and development, embracing technological advancements, fostering a culture of innovation, or enhancing customer experience.

Consider Procter & Gamble's situation. While the company's portfolio is extensive enough to sustain it, it has suffered a loss. Even as you evolve your competitive advantage, remember what sets you apart from other companies and stay true to your mission.

By staying ahead of the curve and actively evolving their competitive advantage, businesses can remain adaptable in an ever-changing market.

Gaining a competitive advantage is also essential for sustainable success. It sets a business apart from rivals while driving growth, profitability, and customer loyalty, making it the key to staying ahead in this highly competitive business world.

Super Hack 18 | Consistency Is Key
We can learn from what these companies have done well

There are invaluable entrepreneurial lessons from three iconic fast-food chains: McDonald's, Starbucks, and Chick-fil-A. These industry giants have mastered the art of consistency, revolutionizing customer experiences, and creating strong brand recognition. From McDonald's unwavering consistency to Starbucks' inviting atmosphere and Chick-fil-A's exceptional customer service, each chain offers unique insights into building a successful business.

> **Self-Assessment Questions:**
>
> 1. How effectively have you established and maintained consistency in your brand identity, product quality, and customer service? Can customers rely on a consistent experience each time they interact with your business, fostering trust and loyalty?
>
> 2. In creating the customer experience, have you considered going beyond the product itself, focusing on elements like ambiance, comfort, and customer engagement? How can you enhance the overall experience to make customers feel valued and encourage repeat visits?
>
> 3. Reflecting on your commitment to exceptional customer service, do you have systems in place to efficiently handle peak times and high customer volumes?

Super Hack 18 | Consistency Is Key
We can learn from what these companies have done well

Fast food chains have revolutionized the business world with their ability to provide consistent products and exceptional customer experiences. Their success can be attributed to various factors, including effective branding, consistent quality, and strong customer service.

Let's look into three renowned fast-food chains - McDonald's, Starbucks, and Chick-fil-A - and delve into a few of the entrepreneurial lessons that can be learned from their remarkable achievements.

McDonald's

One of the key lessons entrepreneurs can learn from McDonald's[32] is the power of consistency and brand recognition. Regardless of the location, McDonald's maintains a similar standard of quality and service, offering customers the same experience every time they visit.

This consistency builds trust among consumers, who know exactly what to expect from the brand, whether in New York or Tokyo. As an entrepreneur, it is crucial to establish a strong brand identity and consistently deliver on your promises to foster customer loyalty and build a solid reputation.

From my experience, I would suggest customer service often suffers at McDonald's. I find I provide more hospitality to the person serving me or taking my order than they offer me; I often hear the retort "yup" to my "thank you."

Contrast this with Chick-fil-A, where a "thank you" is always met with "my pleasure."

Starbucks

Starbucks[33] has not only become synonymous with specialty coffees but also with an inviting and comfortable atmosphere that encourages people to stay and enjoy their beverages ("your third place.).

Entrepreneurs can learn from Starbucks' commitment to consistency in their drinks' taste and presentation, ensuring customers receive the same high-quality experience across all locations. Additionally, Starbucks' focus on creating cozy environments with comfortable seating and free Wi-Fi has transformed their stores into popular social venues and workspaces.

> Entrepreneurs should strive to create an experience beyond the product, making customers feel valued and providing an inviting and welcoming atmosphere that encourages repeat visits.

Not only does Starbucks offer a consistent, high-quality service, but on a recent visit with my dog (Luna), they engaged with her and provided her with a free pup cup (now, she is conditioned when she rides by their store to think we are going there for a treat – free for her and an expensive drink for me).

Chick-fil-A

Chick-fil-A [34] has set itself apart in the fast-food industry through its exceptional customer service and strong emphasis on values. The chain is known for its friendly and courteous staff, who consistently go above and beyond to ensure customer satisfaction.

This dedication to outstanding service has helped Chick-fil-A build a fiercely loyal customer base. Furthermore, the company's commitment to its values, such as closing on Sundays to prioritize employees' well-being, resonates with customers and establishes trust.

Entrepreneurs should prioritize exceptional customer service and uphold values that align with their target audience. By doing so, they can create a strong bond with customers and foster long-term success.

Have you ever had to navigate the drive-thru lane at Chick-fil-A at a peak time of day?

They do it right: there is a system to their madness, and they efficiently service hundreds of hungry customers at each location on a personalized level by having humans with mobile ordering devices to supplement kiosk ordering, offering sauce stations to get your condiments before order pick-up, and often delivering food directly to your car window to speed things up.

Fast food chains like McDonald's, Starbucks, and Chick-fil-A have successfully implemented varied strategic approaches to consistency and brand recognition.

Entrepreneurs can apply valuable lessons from these industry giants to their ventures. Success in any industry is not solely about the products served but rather the holistic experience that customers receive and how the customer is made to feel special, unique, and valued.

Super Hack 19 | The Do's of Innovation
3 fundamental pillars of successful innovation

Guiding businesses on the path to growth, competitive advantage, and customer satisfaction are essential principles. By adopting a strategic approach and adhering to core operating principles, organizations can unlock the full potential of innovation. We begin by emphasizing the importance of creating a user-centered experience, drawing inspiration from industry leaders like Wegmans and Disney, who prioritize employee satisfaction to elevate customer interactions.

> **Self-Assessment Questions:**
>
> 1. How well do you prioritize creating a user-centered experience in your innovation process? Are you actively engaging in user research and continuous feedback collection to understand your target audience's needs, desires, and pain points throughout the development stages?
>
> 2. To what extent do you encourage a collaborative culture within your organization for fostering innovation? Are you actively promoting open communication and cross-functional collaboration to bring together diverse perspectives for problem-solving?
>
> 3. How effectively do you balance pushing the boundaries of innovation with staying true to your company's core competencies and brand essence? Are you mindful of avoiding the "Shiny Object Syndrome" and straying too far from your strengths?

Super Hack 19 | The Do's of Innovation
3 fundamental pillars of successful innovation

Innovation can be the lifeblood of any successful business – driving growth, competitive advantage, and customer satisfaction – if you do it right. You can achieve meaningful innovation by taking a strategic approach and adhering to certain core operating principles.

Create a user-centered experience.

One of the fundamental pillars of successful innovation is to design around the user. Successful grocery store chain Wegmans[35] has high-ranking customer satisfaction because it focuses on keeping employees happy.

When the employees are happy, they engage well with customers and elevate the user experience.

> Involving the user early on in development is a great way to uncover valuable insights. Prototyping and iterative testing allow for rapid refinement, ensuring your innovation meets expectations.

This logic model follows Disney's Leadership Chain of Excellence – create a culture of care for cast members, and they'll deliver nothing short of excellence to guests.

By understanding your target audience's needs, desires, and pain points, you can create an experience that resonates with them.

To resonate with them, you'll need to conduct user research, engage in empathy mapping, and gather feedback at every stage of development.

Even better, you can exceed their expectations and foster loyalty by continuously seeking feedback and iteration based on their insights.

Seek other perspectives.

Collaborative efforts foster true innovation. Cross-functional teams and diverse perspectives unlock fresh ideas and novel approaches to problem-solving.

You can harness your organization's collective intelligence by fostering a culture of open communication and encouraging the sharing of ideas.

This quote by Anish Kapoor encompasses this well: **"All ideas grow out of other ideas."**

Sharing allows you to combine disparate ideas and connect the dots to find those breakthrough innovations.

It's critical to remember that collaboration [36] extends beyond internal teams. Working with customers, suppliers, and competitors will create a ripe environment for new perspectives and insights. Seeking external partnerships and engaging in co-collaboration allows you to leverage the strengths of different stakeholders to create transformative experiences for customers.

This collaborative mindset enriches the innovation process and enhances the chances of delivering customers a "wow" experience.

Stay true to your brand essence.

Innovation is rooted in understanding your company's capabilities and core competencies. While pushing boundaries and exploring new possibilities is essential, it's equally important to recognize your limitations.

Many entrepreneurs fall victim to Shiny Object Syndrome,[37] where they stray too far from core competencies, diluting the brand and compromising the quality of the company's offerings. Just look at what happened to General Electric when it went on an acquisition binge only to reverse course and shed these new acquisitions to narrow its focus and simplify operations, losing billions in value and market cap.

Innovation initiatives should align with your company's strengths and expertise to allow for focused and impactful innovation. By leveraging your existing resources, knowledge, and experience, you can build on your competitive advantage and achieve sustainable growth.

Finally, staying true to your core values and mission ensures that innovation is a strategic enabler, complementing your overall business strategy.

Innovation is a dynamic and transformative force that can drive businesses to new heights. By following the do's of innovation, you'll be well-equipped to navigate an ever-evolving landscape and build a *thriving* future for your organization.

Super Hack 20 | The Don'ts of Innovation
Avoid falling victim to these common mistakes

Avoid fatal pitfalls on the path to successful innovation, and recognize that while innovation drives progress, it's fraught with challenges. With statistics suggesting a high failure rate for product innovations, it's imperative to avoid common missteps that can impede growth. Caution against settling for mediocrity in team composition, stress the importance of assembling an innovation-focused team that aligns with the company's values, and advocate for exploration and iteration rather than latching onto initial ideas.

> **Self-Assessment Questions:**
>
> 1. How effectively do you prioritize teamwork and cultural alignment when building your innovation-focused team? Do you actively assess skills and abilities that may not emerge from traditional interviews to ensure a successful fit?
>
> 2. To what extent do you encourage an open-minded approach to idea exploration within your innovation process? Are you prone to falling in love with the first idea that comes to mind, or do you embrace a culture of continual exploration? How well do you engage in brainstorming sessions and seek feedback from team members?
>
> 3. How thoroughly do you validate your innovative products or services before assuming immediate customer adoption? Are you investing adequate time and resources in market research, surveys, and test runs to understand your target audience's needs and preferences?

Super Hack 20 | The Don'ts of Innovation
Avoid falling victim to these common mistakes

Innovation is the lifeblood of progress, driving industries forward and shaping our world. However, the path to successful innovation is challenging, and many organizations stumble due to common pitfalls. To truly thrive in this dynamic landscape, it's crucial to avoid certain traps that can hinder growth and success.
40-90% of all product innovations fail, depending on who you believe.

In other words, if you want to succeed, don't exhibit these innovation bad behaviors.

Bad Behavior #1: Don't settle

A significant driver of innovation is the human element. The right team can spark revolutionary ideas, foster creativity, and bring visions to life. Conversely, a poor hiring decision can have the opposite effect, dragging down the entire innovation process.

When building an innovation-focused team, look for those with the required skills and expertise while matching the company's culture and values. A cohesive team will communicate effectively, collaborate seamlessly, and support each other in pursuing innovation.

It's essential not to settle for employees who don't fit their roles well – despite an impressive resume.

Embrace the journey of trial and error and pivots, as it may lead to unexpected and superior solutions.

Consider your culture and how employees truly promote your company's mission and values. P&G [38] uses online assessments with potential applicants to measure skills and abilities that generally do not emerge from interviews. The questions and activities allow the company to see who would be successful in a position there.

Bad Behavior #2: Don't just go with the first idea

"Eureka!" moments are exhilarating but don't always lead to the best ideas. A common pitfall in innovation is falling in love with the first idea that comes to mind and sticking to it doggedly.

True innovation requires exploration, iteration, and an open mind.

After the initial burst of inspiration, take the time to analyze and refine your ideas. Engage in brainstorming sessions, seek feedback from team members, and conduct thorough market research.

Remember, successful innovation often involves pivoting and adapting along the way. As Thomas Edison [39] famously said, "I have not failed. I've just found 10,000 ways that won't work."

Bad Behavior #3: Don't assume customers will buy immediately

Innovation [40] can be thrilling, and entrepreneurs may be tempted to believe that their revolutionary product or service will immediately resonate with consumers. However, assuming that buyers will flock to your innovation without proper market validation is a dangerous mindset.

Before launching a new product, invest time and resources in market research and validation. Understand your target audience's needs, pain points, and preferences. Conduct surveys, focus groups, and test runs to gather feedback and insights.

This data-driven approach will help refine and tailor your innovation to meet real-world demands. Additionally, be prepared for a gradual adoption curve, as even the most groundbreaking innovations often take time to gain traction in the market.

Most of all, there is more to innovation than just products. It can be a cadre of other types – process, customer experience, brand, channel, or business model.

While large companies [41] often struggle with critical dimensions of innovation – speed, cultural transformation, resource allocation, risk-taking, and a "more to lose" mindset – metrics-based entrepreneurial businesses often lack focus, urgency, and resources (that is, they run out of money!).

Successful innovation requires a delicate balance of creativity, strategy, and adaptability. By avoiding the common *don'ts* of innovation, you can foster an environment that nurtures groundbreaking ideas and propels your organization toward lasting success.

Remember, the innovation journey is as vital as the destination, so embrace the process and keep pushing the boundaries of what's possible.

Super Hack 21 | Get Your Head in the Game
Three strategies for a growth mindset

While entrepreneurship may seem glamorous, it demands a unique approach and mentality. Entrepreneurs must embrace ownership of their challenges, seeing them as opportunities for growth and innovation rather than obstacles. Additionally, they must be action-oriented, avoiding overthinking to take decisive steps toward their goals. Successful entrepreneurs are willing to take calculated risks, leveraging market research and strategic thinking to make informed decisions. By embodying these principles, aspiring entrepreneurs can cultivate the mindset necessary to thrive.

> **Self-Assessment Questions:**
>
> 1. How effectively do you take ownership of challenges in my role, regardless of whether you caused them or not? Do you see problems as opportunities for growth and innovation, and are you proactive in creating Impactful solutlons?
>
> 2. Can you balance planning and acting effectively, or do you tend to overthink and hesitate before taking steps? How do you draw inspiration from stories of entrepreneurs who have turned their ideas into reality by taking calculated action?
>
> 3. Do you approach risk-taking in your entrepreneurial pursuits with a strategic mindset, considering risks should be accounted for by thorough research and analysis? How do you demonstrate resilience in the face of setbacks, and how do you leverage your understanding of the target market and industry trends to make informed decisions?

Super Hack 21 | Get Your Head in the Game
Three strategies for a growth mindset

Entrepreneurship is a dynamic endeavor in which individuals embark on a journey to build something extraordinary. Following a vision or idea may seem glamorous from afar, but the entrepreneurial path demands a unique mindset and approach to navigate it effectively.

It takes a growth mindset, and I suggest three strategies for developing it.

Take ownership.

Entrepreneurs thrive on taking ownership[42] of their challenges – whether they're at fault or not – rather than shying away from them. What do I mean by that?

They own the problem. It may have been caused by someone or something else, but they make the problem theirs to solve.

> Instead of blaming external factors, successful entrepreneurs see problems as opportunities for growth and innovation. They control their destiny by owning the problem and empowering themselves to create impactful solutions.

Entrepreneurs understand that success comes not by running from problems but by confronting them head-on.

In addition to owning their challenges, entrepreneurs take on challenges they see. A problem needing a solution is an opportunity, not an obstacle. They possess a keen eye for identifying gaps in the market, unmet needs, or emerging trends that can be transformed into viable business ventures.

Possibly *their* viable business ventures.

This hunger to solve problems allows entrepreneurs to disrupt industries and create value where it was previously overlooked. It will enable them to succeed where others fail.

Just think about how often you've met someone with a great idea but didn't act on it.

They didn't choose to own the challenge – but later saw their idea as a product in the marketplace: someone else's product and their regret. Take ownership of your challenges – and take on the challenges you see.

Take action.

Many people get into their heads and overthink every aspect of their business before starting. They psyche themselves out.

Planning is essential, but acting is even more so. Recently, Entrepreneur magazine captured 15 different stories of 20-year-olds who built million-dollar businesses. Each identified a problem, devised a business idea, and made it happen. They did not overthink or hesitate.

Use their stories [43] to inspire you to turn your ideas into reality.

It's also always possible to get started on a new idea. Many people in their 50s and 60s are also forming startups.

An essential aspect of the entrepreneur mindset is setting clear and ambitious goals. However, more than merely defining these goals is required; the key lies in taking consistent and focused action to achieve them.

Entrepreneurs are doers. They understand that dreams alone cannot build businesses. Instead, they set specific milestones and break them down into actionable steps to make steady progress.

A goal-oriented entrepreneur also possesses resilience in the face of adversity. They acknowledge that setbacks are a part of the journey and treat them as temporary roadblocks rather than permanent road closures. This mindset helps them stay persistent and adapt their strategies to keep moving forward.

Execute on prudent risks.

Risk-taking is an inherent part of entrepreneurship, but it's not about making impulsive decisions. The entrepreneurial mindset is characterized by taking <u>calculated risks</u> [44] – those that have been thoroughly assessed and aligned with potential rewards.

Entrepreneurs understand that staying in their comfort zones won't lead to innovation or growth. Despite the mythology, entrepreneurs are contingent thinkers, often seeing around corners and mitigating perceived and known risks.

One of the best founders I have worked with often had two or three alternative plans if the first didn't work.

He worked diligently to avoid problems in commercializing his medical device, allowing him to anticipate the issues and creatively overcome regulatory, market, and customer setbacks.

These calculated risks are informed by market research, analysis of industry trends, and a deep understanding of the target audience. Entrepreneurs know when to take a leap of faith, backed by solid data and informed intuition.

They are not reckless gamblers but strategic players who weigh the potential outcomes before making pivotal choices.

Not only understanding but leveraging the entrepreneurial mindset is essential for anyone aspiring to enter the world of entrepreneurship. Aspiring entrepreneurs can pave their way to success and make a lasting impact on the world by taking ownership of challenges, being willing to act, and weighing the risks.

Remember, becoming a successful entrepreneur is not just about building a business; it's about embodying a way of thinking and principles that propel you toward greatness.

Super Hack 22 | Cultivate the Entrepreneurial Spirit
3 larger organizational attributes to be more entrepreneurial

There should be strong importance placed on nurturing an entrepreneurial mindset within your organization. Embracing change, taking calculated risks, and challenging the status quo are essential elements of this mindset, enabling companies to innovate and stay ahead of the curve. However, instilling such a mindset requires a deliberate approach. You can create a culture that fosters entrepreneurial thinking and drives future success.

> **Self-Assessment Questions:**
>
> 1. How effectively do you encourage a culture of constructive failure within your organization, where experimentation and risk-taking are celebrated, with setbacks being viewed as opportunities for learning?
>
> 2. What measures do you take to motivate and support your team members, fostering a sense of ownership and entrepreneurial thinking? How do you invest in employee growth through professional development opportunities, mentorship programs, and regular feedback?
>
> 3. In what ways do you encourage the adoption of new execution strategies within your organization, challenging established norms, and promoting fresh perspectives? How do you promote cross-functional collaboration to stimulate the flow of diverse ideas?

Super Hack 22 | Cultivate the Entrepreneurial Spirit
3 larger organizational attributes to be more entrepreneurial

In today's rapidly evolving business landscape, fostering an entrepreneurial mindset within your organization is key to keeping your team's innovative spirit alive. An entrepreneurial mindset will allow your company to embrace change, take calculated risks, and challenge the status quo — making you ultra-competitive in the marketplace. However, paving the way for a more entrepreneurial organization requires a tailored approach.

By failing forward, providing robust support for your team, and quickly adopting new strategies, you can instill an entrepreneurial mindset that guarantees future success for your organization.

"Constructive" failure

Failure has long been feared in the corporate world. However, understanding that it's inevitable allows you to control it by "failing forward" [45] or turning what would otherwise be failures into opportunities. Encouraging your team to step outside their comfort zones and explore unconventional solutions helps create a culture where experimentation is celebrated, even if it results in setbacks or mistakes. This mindset shift can lead to breakthroughs that would have otherwise remained hidden beneath the fear of failure. By failing forward, you transform missteps into stepping stones that lead to success by analyzing your failures and extracting lessons rather than letting them push you back.

Combat your fear of failure by remembering Jeff Bezos's axiom: "Launch when 70% ready". This serves as a reminder that speed, execution, and a little risk go a long way.

Motivation and support

A workforce that is inspired, motivated, and supported is likely to take ownership of their roles and responsibilities, meaning leaders must invest in employee growth and well-being to foster an entrepreneurial environment. After all, entrepreneurial spirit is simply a mindset.[46] Instead of waiting for change to occur, entrepreneurs venture out and create it. By providing professional development opportunities, mentorship programs, and regular feedback, you can cultivate a sense of ownership for employees and encourage entrepreneurial thinking. This reinforces the message that creativity and risk-taking are valued and appreciated and encourages employees to contribute novel ideas and solutions.

Many organizations need help with inaction or risk aversion, stifling innovation. Don't be afraid to take risks and move your company in a new direction. Remember, history favors the bold, just not the recklessly bold.

Adopt new execution strategies.

Embracing an entrepreneurial ethos requires a departure from traditional execution strategies. You can encourage your team to challenge established norms and explore fresh perspectives, like Starbucks,[47] which encourages employees to create new drinks for a chance to have them sold in stores. There are monthly competitions with different themes, and baristas take it upon themselves to develop creative ideas, prepare drinks, and present them to a panel of judges.

Understanding how to fail forward, providing motivation and support for your team, and adopting new execution strategies will foster a strong entrepreneurial spirit and actively combat organizational paralysis. Integrating these principles into your company culture creates an environment that celebrates innovation, thoughtful risk-taking, and forward-thinking.

> By diversifying approaches and testing new ideas, you create an atmosphere where innovation thrives. Encouraging cross-functional collaboration supports the flow of diverse ideas, which can lead to groundbreaking solutions.

End Notes for Innovation & Entrepreneurship Section

1. Jason Del Rey, "Layoffs, Buyouts, and Rescinded Offers: Amazon's Status as a Top Tech Employer Is Taking a Hit," Vox, December 8, 2022, https://www.vox.com/recode/2022/12/8/23498824/amazon-layoffs-voluntary-buyouts-rescinded-offe rs-reputation.
2. David Schatsky, "Deloitte BrandVoice: Uncertainty And Innovation At Speed," Forbes, accessed September 22, 2023, https://www.forbes.com/sites/deloitte/2021/03/18/uncertainty-and-innovation-at-speed/.
3. *Big Rocks in First | The Art of Manliness*, 2014, https://www.youtube.com/watch?v=0VNmIxkyHd8.
4. Emma Goldberg, "A.I.'s Threat to Jobs Prompts Question of Who Protects Workers," *The New York Times*, May 23, 2023, sec. Business, https://www.nytimes.com/2023/05/23/business/jobs-protections-artificial-intelligence.html.
5. "Global Economics Analyst The Potentially Large Effects of Artificial Intelligence on Economic Growth (BriggsKodnani)," 2023.
6. "A Therapist Speaks: Yes, Loneliness Is a Big Deal," EverydayHealth.com, May 19, 2023, https://www.everydayhealth.com/columns/a-therapist-speaks/us-surgeon-general-vivek-murthy-just-deemed-loneliness-a-public-health-threat/.
7. Paul R. Daugherty, H. James Wilson, and Karthik Narain, "Generative AI Will Enhance — Not Erase — Customer Service Jobs," *Harvard Business Review*, March 30, 2023, https://hbr.org/2023/03/generative-ai-will-enhance-not-erase-customer-service-jobs.
8. Guy Yehiav, "Council Post: Augmented Intelligence: Empowering Humans, Not Replacing Them," Forbes, accessed September 22, 2023, https://www.forbes.com/sites/forbestechcouncil/2019/12/16/augmented-intelligence-empowering-hu mans-not-replacing-them/.
9. Sarah Dégallier-Rochat et al., "Human Augmentation, Not Replacement: A Research Agenda for AI and Robotics in the Industry," *Frontiers in Robotics and AI* 9 (October 4, 2022): 997386, https://doi.org/10.3389/frobt.2022.997386.
10. "6 Pros and Cons of Globalization in Business to Consider," Business Insights Blog, April 1, 2021, https://online.hbs.edu/blog/post/pros-and-cons-of-globalization.
11. "Global Press Release," GEM Global Entrepreneurship Monitor, accessed September 25, 2023, https://www.gemconsortium.org/reports/latest-global-report.
12. "Tokyo's New Rental Umbrella Service Is Perfect for Sudden Showers, Staying Dry on the Cheap," Japan Today, June 11, 2019, https://

japantoday.com/category/features/lifestyle/tokyo%E2%80%99s-new-rental-umbrella-service- is-perfect-for-sudden-showers-staying-dry-on-the-cheap.

13 Gallup Inc, "The Talent for Entrepreneurship," Gallup.com, November 24, 2014, https://news.gallup.com/businessjournal/179531/talent-entrepreneurship.aspx.

14 Edward Russell, "Delta Air Lines Revenues Fully Recovered From Pandemic," Airline Weekly, June 1, 2022, https://airlineweekly.skift.com/2022/06/delta-air-lines-revenues-fully-recovered-from-pandemic/.

15 "What Is The Great Recession? – Forbes Advisor," accessed September 25, 2023, https://www.forbes.com/advisor/investing/great-recession/.

16 E. O. Global, "5 Market Shifts That Could Compromise Your Business (and How to Prepare) - The EO Blog," December 27, 2017, https://blog.eonetwork.org/2017/12/5-market-shifts-compromise-business-prepare/, https://blog.eonetwork.org/2017/12/5-market-shifts-compromise-business-prepare/.

17 "How To Use Pest Analysis Rebranded Video," accessed September 25, 2023, https://cdn.jwplayer.com/previews/P6GwLSSR-5WSyalpf.

18 Taja Dockendorf, "Council Post: A Mix Of Full-Time And Freelance Workers Can Help Your Agency Evolve," Forbes, accessed September 25, 2023, https://www.forbes.com/sites/forbesagencycouncil/2021/08/09/a-mix-of-full-time-and-freelance-workers-can-help-your-agency-evolve/.

19 Adam Ozimek and Christopher Stanton, "Remote Work Has Opened the Door to a New Approach to Hiring," *Harvard Business Review*, March 11, 2022, https://hbr.org/2022/03/remote-work-has-opened-the-door-to-a-new-approach-to-hiring.

20 "6 Stories of Super Successes Who Overcame Failure," Entrepreneur, December 8, 2014, https://www.entrepreneur.com/leadership/6-stories-of-super-successes-who-overcame-failure/240492.

21 "Fear of Failure among Entrepreneurs Worldwide 2022," Statista, accessed September 29, 2023, https://www.statista.com/statistics/268788/fear-of-failure-start-ups-in-leading-economic-nations/.

22 "How Baby Carrots, Birthed by Necessity, Became Big Business," accessed September 29, 2023, https://www.chicagotribune.com/business/ct-business-of-baby-carrots-20160118-story.html.

23 Leonardo Faierman, "Xiaflex's Odd 'Bent Carrot' Ad Sparks Penile Health Awareness," November 17, 2021, https://www.adweek.com/brand-marketing/an-ad-about-penile-health-has-added-new-meaning-to-the-term-bent-carrot/.

24 Susan Peppercorn, "How to Overcome Your Fear of Failure," *Harvard Business Review*, December 10, 2018, https://hbr.org/2018/12/how-to-overcome-your-fear-of-failure.
25 Amy C. Edmondson, "Strategies for Learning from Failure," *Harvard Business Review*, April 1, 2011, https://hbr.org/2011/04/strategies-for-learning-from-failure.
26 Pink, *The Power of Regret*.
27 "Google - About Google, Our Culture & Company News," accessed September 29, 2023, https://about.google/intl/ALL_us/.
28 "Superiority: A Higher Standard of Excellence," Procter & Gamble, accessed December 4, 2023, https://us.pg.com/annualreport2021/superiority-a-higher-standard-of-excellence/.
29 "12 Competitive Advantage Examples (Plus Definition) | Indeed.Com," accessed December 4, 2023, https://www.indeed.com/career-advice/career-development/competitive-advantage-examples.
30 "Warren Buffett Explains His Moat Principle," Yahoo Finance, February 6, 2020, https://finance.yahoo.com/news/warren-buffett-explains-moat-principle-164442359.html.
31 Martin Reeves and Mike Deimler, "Adaptability: The New Competitive Advantage," *Harvard Business Review*, July 1, 2011, https://hbr.org/2011/07/adaptability-the-new-competitive-advantage.
32 Patrick Spenner, "Brand Growth Lessons From McDonald's," Forbes, accessed December 4, 2023, https://www.forbes.com/sites/patrickspenner/2013/06/21/lessons-from-mcdonalds/.
33 "(14) Starbucks | Brand Awareness | Strategy | LinkedIn," accessed December 4, 2023, https://www.linkedin.com/pulse/starbucks-brand-awareness-strategy-jose-furtado/.
34 Paul Jankowski, "How One Chicken Chain Is Winning Big: A Case Study In Sticking To Brand Values," Forbes, accessed December 4, 2023, https://www.forbes.com/sites/pauljankowski/2019/05/30/how-one-chicken-chain-is-winning-big-a-ca se-study-in-sticking-to-brand-values/.
35 Blake Morgan, "100 Of The Most Customer-Centric Companies," Forbes, accessed January 12, 2024, https://www.forbes.com/sites/blakemorgan/2019/06/30/100-of-the-most-customer-centric-companie s/.
36 "How Collaboration Can Help Your Business | Business.Gov.Au," tutorial page, January 10, 2024, https://business.gov.au/planning/innovation/how-collaboration-can-help-your-business.
37 "Do You Have 'Shiny Object' Syndrome? What It Is and How to Beat It," Entrepreneur, February 9, 2017, https://www.entrepreneur.com/living/do-you-have-shiny-object-syndrome-what-it-is-and-how-to/288370.

38. "Assessment-Overviews," Procter & Gamble, accessed January 19, 2024, https://www.pgcareers.com/global/en/assesment-overviews.
39. Nathan Furr, "How Failure Taught Edison to Repeatedly Innovate," Forbes, accessed January 19, 2024, https://www.forbes.com/sites/nathanfurr/2011/06/09/how-failure-taught-edison-to-repeatedly-innova te/.
40. Mark Gottfredson and Keith Aspinall, "Innovation Versus Complexity: What Is Too Much of a Good Thing?," *Harvard Business Review*, November 1, 2005, https://hbr.org/2005/11/innovation-versus-complexity-what-is-too-much-of-a-good-thing.
41. "The Biggest Obstacles to Innovation in Large Companies," *Harvard Business Review*, July 30, 2018, https://hbr.org/2018/07/the-biggest-obstacles-to-innovation-in-large-companies.
42. Matthew Toren, "3 Ways Owning Your Mistakes Will Make You Powerful," Entrepreneur, March 24, 2014, https://www.entrepreneur.com/growing-a-business/3-ways-owning-your-mistakes-will-make-you-po werful/232417.
43. Entrepreneur Staff, "How 15 People in Their 20s Built Million-Dollar Businesses," Entrepreneur, August 24, 2021, https://www.entrepreneur.com/growing-a-business/how-15-people-in-their-20s-built-million-dollar-businesses/380002.
44. Chris Carosa, "Why Successful Entrepreneurs Need To Be Calculated Risk Takers," Forbes, accessed March 1, 2024, https://www.forbes.com/sites/chriscarosa/2020/08/07/why-successful-entrepreneurs-need-to-be-calculated-risk-takers/.
45. Stephen Childs, "Council Post: Failing Forward -- And Why It's OK," Forbes, accessed March 13, 2024, https://www.forbes.com/sites/forbeshumanresourcescouncil/2019/08/23/failing-forward-and-why-its- ok/.
46. Jacquelyn Smith, "How To Keep Your Entrepreneurial Spirit Alive As The Company You Work For Grows," Forbes, accessed March 13, 2024, https://www.forbes.com/sites/jacquelynsmith/2013/10/22/how-to-keep-your-entrepreneurial-spirit-ali ve-as-the-company-you-work-for-grows/.
47. "Starbucks Barista Innovation Challenge," Starbucks Stories, accessed March 13, 2024, https://stories.starbucks.com/stories/2017/behind-scenes-starbucks-barista-innovation-challenge/.

3. Marketing & Branding
In-Brief

Marketing and branding are indispensable to modern business strategies, shaping perceptions, driving consumer engagement, and cultivating brand loyalty. Effective marketing initiatives encompass diverse tactics, from traditional advertising to digital media campaigns, all aimed at enhancing brand visibility and image. Concurrently, branding efforts establish a distinct identity and narrative, distinguishing a company from fierce competition and resonating with target audiences on a deeper level. This section explores how marketing and branding impact consumer behavior and the strategic approaches used by early-stage companies for building enduring brand equity.

Super Hack 23 | Building Authentic & Engaging Customer Relationships
Craft a seamless brand experience across online and offline touchpoints

A single encounter with a business can profoundly impact a customer's perception and loyalty in today's digital age, where online presence is paramount and mastering the art of branding and customer service is essential for success. From defining your brand identity to staying current on industry trends, we'll explore the key strategies to elevate your online marketing and branding efforts.

> **Self-Assessment Questions:**
>
> 1. How effectively does your brand communicate its values and establish trust in the minds of your customers, considering that branding encompasses the entire identity of your business?
>
> 2. To what extent do you embrace collaboration with influencers, industry experts, or complementary businesses to expand your brand's online reach and increase visibility?
>
> 3. How well do you stay current on the latest trends in the digital landscape, including shifts in technology, consumer behavior, and popular platforms, and how does this awareness influence your online marketing and branding strategies to maintain relevance with changes in the digital era?

Super Hack 23 | Building Authentic & Engaging Customer Relationships
Craft a seamless brand experience across online and offline touchpoints

"Customer Service Matters: It's Why I'm Leaving My Ford Dealership," my friend's blog title read.

And when I read about her experience with that brand's service department – mainly with one person in that small unit -- I agreed she *should* quit taking her car there. I'd avoid taking mine if that were my car dealership.

Will her small voice in the digital wilderness garner enough attention to impact that business? You never know.

But what you can know for sure is your brand's *reputation* – and isn't that ultimately what a brand is? – is only as strong as customers' weakest encounter with it, and what they choose to do about it.

While my friend's experience was in-person, her response is online – on her blog and social media platforms.

In today's digital age, online marketing and branding have become essential for businesses of all sizes. With the vast reach and influence of the internet, establishing a robust *positive* online presence is crucial for attracting customers and staying ahead of the competition.

Many companies use an online presence to create entertaining and engaging content to attract potential customers. They make a loyal following (or "tribe"), then advertise their product by following the latest trends. The best brands both customize and personalize their customer experiences. They interact, reinforce, and create calls to action (CTAs).

Let's examine how you can be distinctive in the marketplace by considering some fundamentals.

Branding matters.

Branding[1] is much more than just a logo or a catchy tagline. It encompasses the entire identity and perception of your business in the minds of consumers. Effective branding communicates your values, establishes trust, and creates a memorable experience for your target audience. Professor Jeremy VanAndel at Franklin College said, "Brands are the feelings people have about a thing, and, just like how you feel about your friends and family, those feelings are based on experiences."

A strong brand sets you apart in the competitive online landscape and helps customers recognize and choose your business over others. Consistency in branding across various online platforms, such as your website, social media profiles, and advertising campaigns, is critical to building customer familiarity and loyalty.

However, the online landscape is only part of what you must consider.

As my friend's experience illustrates, the employee receiving a call, standing behind the service counter, or responding to a direct message must reflect those brand standards, too.

Investing in a well-defined brand strategy – and getting buy-in from every team member, too – allows you to establish a long-lasting connection with your audience and differentiate yourself in a crowded marketplace.

Be open to collaboration.

Collaboration is a powerful tool for expanding your online marketing and branding efforts. By partnering with influencers, industry experts, or complementary businesses, you can reach new audiences and increase your brand visibility and exposure.

Influencer marketing, for instance, allows you to tap into the influencer's existing follower base, leveraging their credibility and authority to promote your products or services.

Or consider having industry experts or complementary businesses as special guests in your content or joint live streams. It diversifies your content and introduces your brand to a broader audience.

By embracing collaboration, you can harness the collective power and expertise of others to amplify your brand message and expand your online reach.

There are many instances of backlashes, whether it be celebrities who are fired from the brands they represent, cause-based marketing that regrettably results in brand misalignment, setbacks, "epic fails," or meltdowns. Inc. Magazine's writer Geoffrey James' brand disaster definition[2] insightfully recognized, "A brand disaster[3] is when a company does something *so stupid* that it causes the public's perception of the brand [4] (a.k.a. its "brand image") to turn from positive to negative."

Stay current on trends.

The digital landscape is ever-evolving, and staying up-to-date with the latest trends is crucial for effective online marketing and branding. Advances in technology, shifts in consumer behavior, and emerging platforms all present new opportunities to engage with your target audience.

> For all the attention paid to celebrity endorsements, recent surveys show "brand mascots (like Aflac Duck, Flo from Progressive, and Pillsbury Doughboy) are more effective than celebrities."

If you keep an eye on industry trends, you can adapt your strategies and stay relevant in the rapidly changing online landscape.

Social media platforms constantly evolve, introducing new features and algorithms affecting your brand's visibility. Keeping a pulse on these changes allows you to optimize your social media marketing efforts and maintain a competitive edge.

Moreover, staying current on trends helps you identify new marketing channels and tactics to bring fresh perspectives and growth opportunities to your brand.

Online marketing and branding are indispensable in today's digital era. You can maximize your brand's visibility, engage with your audience effectively, and drive business success.

Remember, in the dynamic world of online digital marketing, embracing change and adapting your strategies are vital to staying ahead of the curve. Build authentic and long-lasting customer relationships, and you'll likely experience long-term growth.

But never forget that customer service – online, via phone, or in person – is branding, too. Even one poor customer service experience can tarnish the brand you're working so hard to build. Each touchpoint is a moment of truth. A single failure point can destroy all the goodwill created.

Super Hack 24 | Memorable Moments
Keep Customers for Life
How to make your customers feel how much you value them

Position yourself in the heart of customer appreciation and value creation, where every interaction shapes the essence of your brand. From the aroma of your store to the personalized gestures that leave a lasting impression, creating an exceptional customer experience can be powerful, memorable, and sticky. Creating a customer-centric culture should always be at the forefront of your mind.

> **Self-Assessment Questions:**
>
> 1. Do you actively seek to understand your customers' needs, preferences, and pain points, and are you continuously gathering valuable insights to improve their experience?
>
> 2. Are you open to experimentation and regularly conducting trials to optimize the customer experience, considering resource constraints and potential risks while focusing on achieving memorable moments?
>
> 3. Have you identified key performance indicators (KPIs) to measure the success of your customer-centric approach, and are you constantly reviewing progress, delegating responsibilities, and making necessary adjustments to enhance performance and satisfaction levels?

Super Hack 24 | Memorable Moments Keep Customers for Life
How to make your customers feel how much you value them

Was it the smell of popcorn drawing clients to the lobby for our latest "surprise and delight"? Or did the timely invitations delivered via Slack or flyers on each hallway door draw everyone to the lobby this afternoon?

We were ready for them. We'd made our counter a movie-theater refreshment stand, with popcorn and kid-friendly add-ons such as gummy bears, M&Ms, and more. On our lobby TV, we played throwback movie footage advertising refreshments. We kept the corn popping and the treats coming.

Why? We were making a memorable moment because we love our entrepreneurial community and want to ensure they have an experience in our facility beyond mere satisfaction. Far beyond mere satisfaction.

We want to create an exceptional customer experience.

And so, we seek to engage, delight, and build long-lasting customer relationships. LinkedIn calls it "Making Customers Feel 'Cared For'" and 'Valued.'"

We like to do that by making the customer experience intentional, memorable, and sticky (and sometimes it includes candy – or ice cream – that does melt in their hands). We want our clients to choose to work in our facilities every day because of the interactions, connections, warmth, and feel of the experiences we orchestrate.

Let's delve into the three essential steps we've discovered to help us make that happen.

Know your customer and know that you know.

First, to create a customer experience that resonates with your target audience, you've got to understand their needs, preferences, and pain points. Active customer discovery can involve conducting market research, collecting feedback, and conversing directly with your customers. (Popcorn and candy are helpful but not required.)

Gathering valuable insights lets you identify patterns and trends that inform your decision-making process.

Then, it would be best if you validated these insights. Validation allows you to test and refine your assumptions. Do this by implementing real-time surveys, focus groups, or prototype testing to gauge customer reactions and validate your ideas.

(Don't gather insights; hurry to implement them all. Instead, do some trial runs and ask, run experiments, ask, ask for feedback. Yes, at least three times, and ask as many people as possible.)

By actively involving your customers throughout the process, you ensure that the experience you eventually create aligns with their expectations, ultimately fostering loyalty and advocacy.

Think about Southwest's meltdown[5] during the holidays in 2023. They tried to use out-of-date technology to solve customers' complaints but missed the human dimension.

> Remember to keep the experience personal. Sometimes, we over-automate experiences at the expense of high-touch activities. High-touch activities can often reinforce critical components of the brand promise.

It backfired in a significant way. Moments of truth came and went.

Anyone who knows me knows I am a student of the customer experience. Informed by benchmark practices from Disney, Starbucks, Ritz-Carlton, Delta, Zappos, Amazon, and many others, I've concluded that the customer experience is a discipline culturally embedded and reinforced in every customer interaction.

Case in point: I was in the Delta Sky Club in Atlanta a few weeks ago. A passenger was recognized for hitting 1 million miles. They congratulated her, gave her a special dessert, and took selfies. They also had a sign on her seat commemorating the special day. The company created an exceptional customer experience that engaged and delighted her (and the rest of us who watched it happen).

Will she remain a devoted customer? I would bet on it. I sure will be.

Did that make her feel cared for and valued? It made ME feel cared for and valued, too – and made me want to remain a Delta faithful and rack up my miles. I have been a Delta loyalist for a long time. I know that when I need them, I can count on them. Case in point – During a potential stay-in-place order during COVID-19, we had kids at our condo in Destin and needed to get them back to Indiana sooner than their scheduled departure date. Delta mobilized and made it happen. No penalties, no change fees, and no sorry, I can't help you. They made it happen, much to me and my wife's relief.

Conduct 'regular' experiments to optimize and orchestrate the experience.

It's essential to ground your aspirations. Conducting "experiments"[6] helps you understand what falls within your scope of capability to grow and sustain that growth. Assess your available resources, including financial, technical, and human capital, and evaluate whether they align with your customer experience goals.

Some of the best advice I know is: **Dream big, start small, and scale fast.** This framework can serve as an essential beacon on the startup journey.

The potential risks and mitigation strategies during the experimentation phase should also be considered. This analysis will enable you to make informed decisions about resource allocation, prioritize initiatives ("sticky and memorable"), and set realistic timelines, budgets, and resource requirements. By conducting periodic experiments, you ensure that your customer experience initiatives are not only desirable but also achievable within the constraints of your organization.

Identify pain points & key performance indicators.

Defining key performance indicators is crucial to measuring the success of your intentional customer experience. These quantifiable metrics help you track progress and evaluate the impact of your efforts. Simply put, what gets measured gets managed.

They could include tracking customer satisfaction scores, encouraging repeat purchase rates, understanding/tracking Happy or Not scores®,[7] using AI to track customer emotions, implementing a secret shopper program, or tracking net promoter scores.

Once you have identified some responsibilities, delegate them to your appropriate team members or departments. Clearly define roles and set expectations, ensuring everyone understands their contribution to the overall customer experience strategy.

Then, regularly review progress against the identified KPIs, provide feedback, and make necessary adjustments to optimize performance.

Consider customer pain points and engineer creative solutions to address or accommodate their needs.

One pain point for our client's guests is that parking on a university campus is impossible. We added three dedicated parking spaces in our closest lot to the building that clients can reserve for use by their VIPs.

This small gesture has led to many selfies since we personalize each VIP sign with individual and company names. We reinforce this inside the building with digital signage (person's name, logo, and company name) reflecting our VIP guests of the day. We want them to feel valued and special. In my Disney Institute training, the facilitator said," We (Disney) are a first-name company. Everyone has a name tag with their name and their hometown."

Creating an intentional customer experience requires a deliberate and systematic approach. You can bring your vision to life.

Remember that the customer should always remain at the center of your strategy, as their satisfaction and loyalty are the cornerstones of sustainable growth.

Embrace these steps, continuously iterate based on feedback, and watch your organization flourish through a customer-centric approach. Loyalty is earned in every interaction and can be lost quickly when the customer's expectation does not live up to the reality of the service delivery promise. There will be mistakes, so fast and immediate service recovery is essential for success.

The sticky takeaway.

Post-COVID, UF Innovate | Accelerate has been doing random acts of kindness, surprise, and delight (what we call "S&D") to evoke emotional connections for our clients and guests.

In addition to this week's popcorn party, our S&D has included an '80s-themed cart moving from offices to labs in our building with staff dressed for that decade, serving clients cookies with classic '80s music.

On May the 4th (be with you), we were a Star Wars-themed entourage delivering treats throughout the building. On another hot day, we "drove" an ice cream "truck" playing the familiar music that lured so many of us as youngsters to beg for cash and dash to the street to meet the ice cream truck.

And, yes, we served individually wrapped ice cream treats, no cash needed. (Received just as eagerly as our younger selves, I think)

We want our clients and guests to love to go to the office. We want them to hear, smell, and taste – in addition to all the great programming and services we offer – the treat is for us to serve them well.

Because, like the smell of popcorn wafting through our building, we want to reach our clients with the fragrance of an exceptional customer experience and the knowledge that we are there for them because we care. Too many entrepreneurs suffer from loneliness, isolation, depression, and anxiety; I know from the reactions I see from our clients how much they feel valued and cared for. It is our privilege to be their trusted advisor, delivering important business-building programs and an essential support partner on their entrepreneurial journey.

Super Hack 25 | Know Your Value
3 key ways to unlock your business's true potential

Understanding the actual value of your business is crucial to ensure long-term success in a competitive market. Drawing from cautionary tales like that of an underbidding real estate company, we explore three crucial aspects: establishing legitimacy, pricing products or services appropriately, and knowing your market. The key lies in continuous adaptation and improvement, ensuring your business remains aligned with market demands and customer expectations.

> **Self-Assessment Questions:**
>
> 1. Have you taken the necessary steps to establish legitimacy for your business, including obtaining relevant licenses, permits, and certifications and building a solid online presence to enhance credibility and trust with customers and stakeholders?
>
> 2. Have you conducted a thorough cost analysis and market research to determine the optimal pricing strategy for your products or services, considering factors like production costs, competition, and customer demand and emphasizing your business's unique value to the market?
>
> 3. Are you continuously monitoring industry trends, consumer preferences, and market dynamics to stay informed about your target market and adapt your business strategies effectively, ensuring that you deliver exceptional value to your customers and position your business for long-term success?

Super Hack 25 | Know Your Value
3 key ways to unlock your business's true potential

When a new real estate company opened in our area, it purposely underbid what other offices offered to get their clients – and sealed its fate. The clients took the lower rate and kept it low by threatening to go elsewhere should the rate change.

Eventually, the company folded, unable to provide the services for what it had hoped was an introductory offer. By undervaluing its service and buying customers, it had undermined its survival.

As an entrepreneur or small business owner, you, too, must understand the actual value of your business so you can make informed decisions and achieve long-term success.

Knowing your business's value lets you establish legitimacy, set *appropriate* prices for your products or services, and effectively navigate your target market with a strong value proposition. Let's explore three key ways to help you unlock your business's potential.

Establish your legitimacy.

To build trust with your customers and stakeholders, you must establish legitimacy. It is vital in a competitive business landscape. You can attract new clients and secure valuable partnerships by showcasing your business's credibility.

Developing a robust online presence and creating positive digital customer interactions through a well-designed website and active social media accounts can further enhance your business's legitimacy. You can build a strong brand image and earn the trust of potential customers by regularly updating your website with relevant (and quality) content and engaging with your audience on social media platforms.

Consider the food truck. My colleague reminds me that the ice cream truck was the original food truck, peddling inexpensive treats to eager children (and adults like herself) in her neighborhood. Food trucks have expanded well beyond ice cream in the past decades, but even as they developed their niche in the restaurant business, they didn't always find themselves welcome. Many people, especially private store owners, considered food trucks a dirty, illegitimate way of conducting business.

However, the Great Recession of 2008 allowed food trucks to shine in a suffering economy. They provided a convenient way for customers to get inexpensive, quality food. Their popularity has steadily grown since then, which further established their legitimacy.

> Establish legitimacy by obtaining the licenses, permits, and certifications relevant to your industry. These credentials demonstrate your compliance with regulations and signify your commitment to quality and professionalism.

We consider ourselves fortunate to have two established food truck parks within walking distance from our building – peddling everything from bagels, pizza, and street tacos to tasty vegan mac and cheese).

But, unfortunately, no ice cream.

Price your product or service accordingly.

How much can you charge so you don't end up like the real estate firm mentioned above?

The <u>U.S. Chamber of Commerce</u>[8] offers step-by-step advice regarding pricing.

You can choose flat-rate, pay-as-you-go, tiered, subscription or membership pricing, or price per user.

You have many ways to determine how much to charge for your product or service and what pricing model is best for you. Remember, the optimal pricing for your product/service requires a careful analysis of multiple factors, including production costs, competition, and customer demand. One of my favorite contemporary thinkers on pricing is Ash Maurya. He has an excellent blog entitled "<u>Experiments in Pricing</u>."[9] When considering the implications of one of the most critical yet challenging decisions you will make, it's worth a look.

Conduct a thorough cost analysis to ensure your pricing strategy aligns with your business's financial goals and operating cost structure. Consider the expenses associated with production, marketing, and overhead costs while also considering the desired profit margin.

Additionally, research your competitors' pricing models to help you position your offerings competitively. Pricing is not solely about undercutting or matching your competitors but also about highlighting your business's unique value to the market.

You should emphasize the features and benefits your product or service offers and advertise your exceptional customer experience, which might allow you to explain why you're looking for premium pricing.

Know your market.

Above all, know your market. This means connecting the dots, nuances, and dynamics to understand how to operate and navigate its complexities successfully.

Understanding your target market is crucial for tailoring your products or services to meet customer needs effectively.

Conduct quality customer discovery and market research[10] to identify your ideal customer profile, demographics, preferences, and purchasing behavior. This knowledge will enable you to create targeted marketing campaigns and refine your business strategies.

Keep a close eye on industry trends and consumer demands, as they can change rapidly. Utilize online tools, surveys, and customer feedback to gather valuable insights about your market. By staying informed about your customers and adapting to their evolving preferences, you can ensure your business remains competitive and relevant.

Keep it on repeat.

Knowing the actual value of your business empowers you to make informed decisions and maximize your potential for success.

By establishing your legitimacy, pricing your products or services accordingly, and understanding your market, you can effectively position your business for growth and long-term profitability.

What if you – like the real estate company I mentioned– offer your product or service for too little? How can you adjust so you don't suffer the same fate?

Do all the above, then increase your price incrementally (and improve your customer service exponentially).

Understanding your business's value is an ongoing journey and a moving target. Continuously evaluate and adapt your strategies to keep up with market dynamics, and always strive to deliver exceptional value to your customers. With a clear understanding of your business, you will be equipped to navigate the ever-changing business landscape and achieve your entrepreneurial potential.

But the trick is to keep it on repeat.

Super Hack 26 | Know Who Wants What You Are Selling
It's the foundation on which your startup succeeds or fails

Understanding your target market is the lifeline for success. You position yourself as an expert by defining your niche and conducting thorough market research. Addressing your audience's pain points directly fosters long-term loyalty and trust. Additionally, knowing who your customer isn't helps focus resources on areas with the highest return on investment. Through market research, customer feedback, and active listening, you can tailor your offerings to resonate deeply with your target audience, unlocking your business's true potential for growth.

Self-Assessment Questions:

1. Have you identified and defined your niche market based on demographics, psychographics, and behavioral patterns to position your business as an expert in that area, building trust and credibility among your target audience?

2. Are you actively listening to your target market to uncover their pain points, challenges, and frustrations, using feedback obtained from surveys, interviews, or social media polls to refine your products or services and directly address the pain points of your customer's experience?

3. Do you have a deep understanding of your target market, and have you identified those individuals or segments who do not fall within it, allowing you to avoid wasting resources on ineffective marketing efforts and focus your time and resources on those most likely to become loyal customers?

Super Hack 26 | Know Who Wants What You Are Selling
It's the foundation on which your startup succeeds or fails

If you're willing to fail – and want to do it fast – ignore everything I say to you today. But if you want your business to succeed? You must start with this.

In the vast sea of consumers, businesses must navigate their way toward success by understanding how to serve their target market. Gaining a deep understanding of the people you aim to help can be the difference between a flourishing business and one that struggles to stay afloat.

By uncovering your target market's needs, desires, and pain points, you can tailor your products or services to meet their specific demands.

But you must be able to answer this: **Who wants what you're selling?**

Here's how you can know.

Find your niche.

You must identify and define your niche to effectively reach your target market. (If you're wondering how to do this, Meredith Hart's post on HubSpot titled "What is a Niche Market? Examples, Benefits & How to Find One" [11] may be helpful.)

As Hart indicates, you can serve the masses and broaden your offerings to make just anyone happy (hard to do!) or find your niche – a specific market segment your business caters to uniquely. By focusing on a niche, you can position yourself as an expert in that area, building trust and credibility among your target audience.

Understanding the characteristics and preferences of your niche will allow you to tailor your marketing efforts and offerings to resonate deeply with this audience.

Uncover pain points.

Successful businesses thrive by providing solutions to their target market's pain points. To truly understand your target market, you must identify their daily challenges, problems, or frustrations. These are their "pain points," by addressing them, you position your business as a problem solver and create value for your customers.

You may hear the lingo "pain, gain, or job-to-be-done," and all relate to how you can help your customer. The last part of the phrase enables you to determine the first two words. "Job-to-be-done" is a framework for understanding customers' needs and motivations. What are they trying to accomplish or solve?

"Pains" are the negative experiences, emotions, risks, or injuries your customer experiences when trying to get the job done. "Gains" are the positive outcomes and benefits they expect, need, or desire when they do the job.

> Conduct through market research[12] to uncover industry gaps, trends, and opportunities. Define your niche based on demographics, psychographics, and behavioral patterns.

You'll need to actively listen and conduct surveys, interviews, or social media polls to gather feedback directly from your target audience. Then, use this information to refine your products or services, ensuring they directly address the pain points of your customer's experience.

You'll establish long-term customer loyalty and gain a competitive edge by alleviating their struggles. "Pain, gain, or job-to-be-done" is the gold standard for startups when solving a pain point.

Journey mapping[13] can be a beneficial tool to uncover pain points in your customer's experiences.

It allows you to see the relationship and understanding between you and your customers throughout the interaction – from when they first hear about your product or service to how they feel after using it. Doing this lets you understand where to improve to ease pain points and sell more effectively.

Know your customer – and who isn't your customer.

While defining your target market is essential, it's equally crucial to identify those who do not fall within it. Not everyone will be perfect for your business, and that's okay.

By understanding who is not in your target market, you can avoid wasting resources on ineffective marketing efforts. Analyze the characteristics and behaviors of those not aligned with your target market and adjust your strategies accordingly.

Instead, focus your time, energy, and resources on those most likely to become loyal customers. Remember, narrowing your focus doesn't limit your opportunities; you're channeling your efforts into the areas that will yield the highest return on investment.

A customer segment is more than an age group, gender, or socio-economic status. Startups must deeply understand and appreciate a customer's operating environment and how their product or service fits their workflow.

Let me give you an example.

A student in my entrepreneurship class thought her potential customer segment was "women over 40." She figured the all-natural beauty product with anti-aging benefits would benefit mature women. She noticed this would be a vast and appealing market. More than 80 million women in the United States are over 40.

The problem was that a market defined this way, while appealing to the number of potential customers, needed to reflect the sub-segment of women over 40 who would be most interested in the product.

Further characteristics needed definition to be actionable. Take a look at these buyer personas[14] for segments of women over 40. You should notice a need to unpack the women segment by looking at "**who she is, what she wants, and why she buys**."

This is more meaningful to the target segment you are trying to serve than age and gender.

Consider the difference in marketing strategies between Equinox and Planet Fitness.[15] Both are gyms – but on opposite sides of the spectrum.

Equinox is known for its wide range of equipment, classes, and personal training; its members want to work out regularly and lift weights.Planet Fitness is a "judgment-free zone" for beginners who want to start getting into the gym; standard equipment and rules are implemented to make everyone feel welcome.

The overarching idea in today's hack is this: **Know who wants what you're selling**.

If you know who they are, you can tailor your products, services, and marketing strategies to resonate with your customers more deeply.

Embrace the power of market research, customer feedback, and active listening to refine your offerings and establish a strong connection with your target audience. Investing time and effort into understanding your target market unlocks the key to business success and drives long-term growth.

Most startups skip or do an incomplete job of customer discovery.[16] It is no accident that lack of product-market fit is a pivotal contributor to false starts and early failure for startups. Take the time to get this foundational step right. Skip it at your peril. **(Please start here).**

End Notes to Marketing & Branding Section

1. Kristopher Jones, "Council Post: The Importance Of Branding In Business," Forbes, accessed September 25, 2023, https://www.forbes.com/sites/forbesagencycouncil/2021/03/24/the-importance-of-b randing-in-business/.
2. Geoffrey James, "The Biggest Business Disasters of 2019," Inc.com, December 18, 2019, https://www.inc.com/geoffrey-james/had-a-rough-year-well-these-5-brands-had-ye ar-from-hell.html.
3. Geoffrey James, "Top 8 Brand Disasters of 2014," Inc.com, December 4, 2014, 88, https://www.inc.com/geoffrey-james/top-8-brand-disasters-of-2014.html.
4. Geoffrey James, "Top 10 Rebrand Disasters of All Time," Inc.com, November 2, 2015, https://www.inc.com/geoffrey-james/top-10-rebrand-disasters-of-all-time.html.
5. Camila Domonoske, "5 Things to Know about Southwest's Disastrous Meltdown," *NPR*, December 30, 2022, sec. Business, https://www.npr.org/2022/12/30/1146377342/5-things-to-know-about-southwests-di sastrous-meltdown.
6. Blake Morgan, "20 Fresh Examples Of Customer Experience Innovation," Forbes, accessed September 25, 2023, https://www.forbes.com/sites/blakemorgan/2019/10/21/20-fresh-examples-of-custo mer-experience-innovation/.
7. "Stop Guessing. Get Customer Feedback Platform That Works | HappyOrNot®," HappyOrNot, April 13, 2023, https://www.happy-or-not.com/en/.
8. Jacqueline Medina, "How to Price Your Product," https://www.uschamber.com/co/, June 2, 2021, https://www.uschamber.com/co/start/strategy/how-to-price-your-product.
9. "Experiments in Pricing," LEANSTACK Blog, February 16, 2010, https://blog.leanstack.com/experiments-in-pricing/.
10. YEC, "Council Post: 7 Types Of Market Research And How To Improve Them," Forbes, accessed September 29, 2023, https://www.forbes.com/sites/theyec/2022/12/19/7-types-of-market-research-and-h ow-to-improve-them/.
11. "What Is a Niche Market? Examples, Benefits & How to Find One," February 1, 2023, https://blog.hubspot.com/sales/niche-market.
12. "How to Do Market Research: A Guide and Template," accessed October 23, 2023, https://blog.hubspot.com/marketing/market-research-buyers-journey-guide.

13 "Your Ultimate Guide to Customer Journey Mapping," Qualtrics, accessed October 23, 2023, https://www.qualtrics.com/experience-management/customer/customer-journey-m apping/.
14 Sydney Fulkerson, "The Top Five Consumer Segments of Women Over 40," MediaVillage, February 25, 2016, https://www.mediavillage.com/article/the-top-five-consumer-segments-of-women-o ver-40/.
15 Mallory Schlossberg, "The Fastest-Growing Gym in America Has $10 Memberships and Gives out Free Pizza, Bagels, and Candy," Business Insider, accessed October 23, 2023, https://www.businessinsider.com/planet-fitnesss-business-profile-2015-10. [16] "HBSRock-Customer-Discovery-Final.Pdf," accessed October 23, 2023, https://entrepreneurship.hbs.edu/Documents/Session%20Summary/HBSRock-Cus tomer-Discovery-Final.pdf.

4. Personal & Business Development
In Brief

Personal and business development are intertwined journeys toward growth, fulfillment, and success. While personal development focuses on enhancing individual skills, mindset, and well-being, business development entails strategically expanding and improving organizational capabilities, processes, and outcomes. Both are essential for navigating the complexities of business and fostering resilience, adaptability, and innovation. From honing leadership abilities to mastering new technologies, continuous improvement is necessary. This section explores how personal and business development can have transformative potential and offers insights into strategies for achieving excellence in both realms.

Super Hack 27 | Positive Well-being Makes You & Your Team Healthier
Nurturing a holistic approach to workplace well-being

In today's fast-paced world, full of uncertainty and stressful situations, the importance of employee well-being cannot be overstated. We can explore practical strategies for nurturing physical, intellectual, and emotional health in the workplace by drawing insights from various disciplines, including psychology, management, and personal development. From promoting stability to fostering continuous learning and professional growth, each facet contributes to building resilient and engaged teams.

> **Self-Assessment Questions:**
>
> 1. How effectively do you prioritize physical health and wellness within your work routine, and what steps have you taken to ensure a healthier lifestyle, both in and outside the workplace?
>
> 2. Regarding intellectual growth and development, how do you actively seek learning opportunities and encourage continuous learning within your team or organization, considering the importance of staying updated with industry trends?
>
> 3. Regarding emotional and spiritual well-being, how do you foster a positive company culture, encourage social connections, and promote work-life integration to enhance job satisfaction and workplace engagement among your team members?

Super Hack 27 | Positive Well-being Makes You & Your Team Healthier
Nurturing a holistic approach to workplace well-being

Prioritizing employee health and wellness is crucial for creating a positive and productive – and dare I say, happy? -- work environment. The Yale Happiness course [1] shares three simple secrets to happiness: sleep, gratitude, and helping others.

Those three secrets align with physical, intellectual, and emotional/spiritual health, which can improve job satisfaction, reduce absenteeism, and, ultimately, increase productivity. And since a McKinsey Global Institute [2] report revealed "the average employee spends just 39 percent of their day accomplishing role-specific, productive tasks", we all can do better. Increasing that percentage of productivity must be a top priority.

But how?

Author Matthew Kelly captured The Rhythm of Life: Living Every Day with Passion & Purpose nearly a decade ago. [3] He encouraged readers to become the best version of themselves, emphasizing that who you are is more important than what you do.

Indeed, we can explore our well-being in terms of physical, intellectual, emotional, and spiritual health. We can live happier and healthier lives by emphasizing these life dimensions. The program tries to cut through life's clutter and focus on living a life of "passion, purpose, and energy."

We must do that for ourselves and create avenues for our employees to do it themselves.

How exactly do we do that?

By emphasizing physical health.

President John F. Kennedy believed, "Physical fitness is one of the most important keys to a healthy body and the basis of dynamic and creative intellectual activity."

Companies can offer various wellness programs, such as gym memberships, fitness classes, stress management, sleep quality, mindfulness, or on-site workout facilities. Providing healthy food options and encouraging regular breaks for physical activity during the workday can also be helpful.

I work hard to get 8,000 to 10,000 steps a day, read nightly before bed, eat lighter dinners, and recently, tried to integrate some intermittent fasting into my routine (starting with 12 hrs. working my way to 16 hrs.)

But what about remote workers? A 2021 survey[4] concluded, "The average remote worker commutes just 16 steps from their bed to their workstation." This reality sounds the alarm bells for remote workers' potential well-being and activity/mobility levels.

It reminds us to use a team-based approach to well-being while developing our mutual support and accountability network so no one "goes it alone."

By engaging in your intellectual health.

Providing continued learning and professional development opportunities can benefit the employees and the company. Training programs, workshops, and conferences can help employees develop new skills and stay current with industry trends.

It has been my long-held belief that in business incubation programs, one of the most important things we do is to offer our clients knowledge (ability to connect dots), our connections, and access to resources. It is my I invest in our team by attending conferences, gaining new credentials (we recently became certified in Entrepreneurial Mindset Profile), and making community site visits to the startup ecosystems to learn what is working, what is not working, and how different entrepreneurial support organizations unlock value for their clients and community.

Individual training has never been more accessible with online platforms like LinkedIn Learning and Google Career Certificates. Encouraging participation in activities such as book clubs (my favorite is the Next Big Idea Club) [5] or discussions on industry-related topics can also promote intellectual growth and provide networking opportunities.

By nurturing your emotional and spiritual health.

Companies can provide resources for stress management and mindfulness practices, such as meditation or yoga classes. Encouraging employees to take breaks and disconnect from work outside of office hours can also aid in promoting healthy work-life integration.

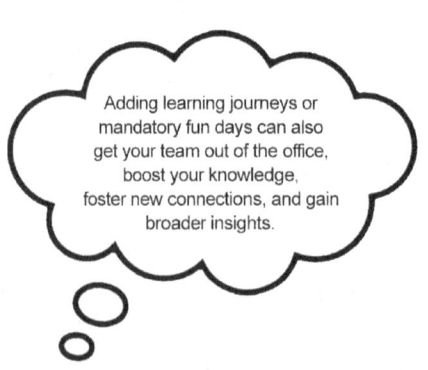

> Adding learning journeys or mandatory fun days can also get your team out of the office, boost your knowledge, foster new connections, and gain broader insights.

Finding that integration is easier said than done. Scheduling your day is vital in finding the right time to take a step away from work guilt-free and truly relax.

Additionally, promoting a positive company culture through team-building activities, social connections, and events can create community, improve job satisfaction, and increase workplace engagement.

At UF Innovate | Accelerate, we have mandatory fun days where we discover more about our university and community, social service projects where we might cook a meal for families of sick children at the Ronald McDonald House, and learning journeys where we know and apply new skills and make new connections.

I always think about Gallup's Q12[6] survey, which measures employee engagement using 12 essential items, and the surprise statement No. 10: "I have a best friend at work."

For a long time, I never knew No. 10 was one of the most positively correlated questions to predicting performance and having a more profound affiliation with your team members. Gallup recognizes that managers can't manufacture such friendships, but they can create opportunities for their colleagues to get to know each other.

Sharing stories and socializing together when it won't disrupt your production could be vital in developing such "best friend" relationships. Moving the needle on this question can improve engagement scores, and many highly engaged ventures achieve higher relative profits.

Key takeaways

Prioritizing employee well-being should be a top priority for companies looking to create a positive and productive work environment. By offering resources and initiatives that promote physical, intellectual, and emotional/spiritual health, companies can build stronger and more resilient teams while helping individuals reach their full potential and become the best version of themselves."

Encouraging healthy work-life integration and promoting a positive company culture can help employees feel valued and supported, leading to a more engaged and motivated workforce.

Our team does this by doing "step" challenges monthly to gear up for a twice-yearly university-wide walking competition. Through the Walker Tracker[7] app, we have explored many fun places like Japan, Australia, the Caribbean, and many other exotic locations around the globe. Through formal university-wide competitions and internal challenges, we have had numerous ways to build camaraderie and support for one another.

But more importantly, we have learned more about each other and our clients, gotten to know each other more personally, and nurtured our commitment to each other to serve and support our business builders.

Super Hack 28 | Grit Is an Elixir
What came first...the Grit or the successful entrepreneur?

Success often hinges not just on brilliant ideas or favorable circumstances but on an intangible quality that sets successful entrepreneurs apart – Grit. Grit embodies passion, perseverance, and resilience, driving individuals to overcome obstacles, embrace challenges, and achieve their goals. It can be used better to navigate the ups and downs of the business world.

> **Self-Assessment Questions:**
>
> 1. Do you regularly celebrate and take stock of your past achievements, milestones, and positive feedback from customers or clients to boost morale and gain valuable insights for future growth?
>
> 2. Have you recently taken the time to reconnect with your initial motivation and core purpose for starting your business? Do you actively use these sources of inspiration to reignite your enthusiasm and drive, particularly during periods of stagnation or adversity?
>
> 3. When facing setbacks or a loss of momentum in your business, do you analyze your actions to prioritize self-care activities that rejuvenate you to face challenges with renewed energy and determination?

Super Hack 28 | Grit Is an Elixir
What came first...the Grit or the successful entrepreneur?

A small school soccer team celebrated its "perfect" first season: all losses.

Even though the score didn't reflect it, the team had improved, but that wasn't enough. The players didn't quit. Instead, they worked together during the off-season to improve their skills. During the long, hot summer months, they committed to practice – together and on their own.

The perfect season they celebrated the following year was genuinely perfect.

They are a picture of true Grit, knuckling down, giving their all (and then some), and digging deep to become better than they were before against all odds.

In entrepreneurship, the path to success is filled with challenges and setbacks. It takes more than a brilliant idea or a stroke of luck to thrive in a dynamic, ever-changing business environment.

It takes Grit. Resilience.

It is the one essential quality that sets successful entrepreneurs apart.

Grit, an internal quality encompassing passion, perseverance, and the ability to withstand adversity (setbacks, seemingly insurmountable obstacles), is the driving force that propels normal individuals to do extraordinary things to achieve their long-term goals.

Many believe that newer generations entering the workforce[8] rely too heavily on instant information, opportunities, and gratification, which can make them miss out on creating great things for themselves they might have done if they were more patient and had more Grit.

I believe it isn't just newer generations. Ample evidence suggests that more and more people across all generations are unwilling to delay gratification. They want instantaneous results. This "du jour" mindset is why many people who encounter early setbacks give up.

Grit comes from within.

However, Grit is only a tangible asset that can be acquired over time. It is an internal quality within the entrepreneurial spirit. It is a mindset that embraces challenges as opportunities for growth, learning, and transformation.

Can you develop "grit"?

Indeed, do hard things. Set goals out of reach or outside your comfort zone. Reach them. When bad things happen, think beyond this minute, this hour, day, or week, and react from a lifelong perspective. Think and respond like a more mature you.

(And try those one at a time. You can find some tools and suggestions here.)[9] Successful entrepreneurs can remain resilient despite failure, setbacks, and rejection. They view obstacles as stepping stones, fueling their determination to overcome difficulties, adjust and adapt to changing circumstances, and connect disparate dots to advance their learning and insights.

Grit requires a deep-rooted belief in oneself and an unwavering commitment to long-term goals. It reminds me of the opening line of a book I read in high school, The **Road Less Traveled** by M. Scott Peck. He said, "Life is difficult. *Discipline is the basic tool we require to solve life's problems." When speaking of delayed gratification,* Peck opined, "Delaying gratification is a process of scheduling the pain and pleasure of life to enhance the pleasure of life in such a way as to enhance the pleasure by meeting and experiencing the pain first and getting it over with. It is the only decent way to live."

Entrepreneurs with Grit possess a strong sense of self-efficacy, recognizing their capabilities and using failures as learning experiences.

"... Grit grows as we figure out our life philosophy, learn to dust ourselves off after rejection and disappointment, and learn to tell the difference between low-level goals that should be abandoned quickly and higher-level goals that demand more tenacity," said pioneering psychologist Angela Duckworth.[10]

I think she describes this quality perfectly.

Grit is why many serial entrepreneurs do it again, again, and again. Grit is why entrepreneurs who experience significant setbacks try again, again, and again.

Passion and perseverance "power" long-term goals.

Passion and perseverance are two crucial components of Grit.

Successful entrepreneurs understand that success rarely comes overnight; it results from consistent hard work and dedication. They embrace the idea of delayed gratification and are willing to endure short-term sacrifices to pursue their vision. Whether working long hours, making tough decisions, or navigating uncertain waters, gritty entrepreneurs stay the course and refuse to give up.

Maybe you know the story about Bill Gates starting Microsoft.[11] This successful entrepreneur started to nurture his passion for computers when he was 13 and continued growing his skillset. In 1975, he co-founded Microsoft with Paul Allen – and the immediate result wasn't success.

It led to financial crises.

But they persevered. They pursued their goals passionately, and in 1980, Microsoft signed a contract to work with IBM. Within a year, Microsoft officially grew to become a Microsoft Corporation.

Setbacks "cement" success.

Have you ever prayed to be more patient? God doesn't suddenly grant you the gift of patience. No. He sends you the "gift" of trials *requiring* your patience. And you develop that character through experience.

Likewise, Grit cannot be acquired instantaneously; it is honed over time through experience and survival. By facing challenges, you build resilience and adaptability. Each setback or obstacle presents an opportunity to learn, grow, and improve.

Gritty entrepreneurs understand that failure is not a permanent condition but a temporary setback on the path to success.

More than anything else I've seen in my tenure, Grit separates successful entrepreneurs from business builders going through the motions.

Do you have what it takes?

Grit is the unwavering determination, passion, and resilience that fuels successful entrepreneurs on their journey to achievement. It is an internal quality that enables individuals to embrace challenges, persevere in adversity, and navigate the ever-changing and dynamic entrepreneurship landscape.

Cultivating and harnessing the power of Grit can be a defining factor in entrepreneurial success.

By accumulating experience, you can develop a mental toolkit to face future challenges. That's how you can learn to think creatively, pivot quickly, and make sound decisions amidst enormous uncertainty.

Even if you must go through a "perfect" season of failure to get there.

Be gritty.

Super Hack 29 | Who Wrote the Rule That Funding Has to Come with Giving Up Ownership of Your Company?
Steps and tips for raising capital without promising away your future earnings

What if the traditional rule of giving up ownership in exchange for funding didn't have to apply to you? What if crowdfunding offered a viable alternative, empowering you to harness collective support while retaining control of your vision? Crowdfunding can allow you to explore new startup benefits, focus on essential steps to launch a successful campaign, and transform the entrepreneurial landscape.

> **Self-Assessment Questions:**
>
> 1. Have you explored alternative funding options, such as crowdfunding, to raise capital for your early-stage venture, challenging the conventional notion that funding must involve giving up ownership of your company?
>
> 2. Are you familiar with the benefits of crowdfunding for startups, including access to a broader pool of potential investors, market validation, and increased marketing and exposure?
>
> 3. Have you taken the necessary steps to prepare for a crowdfunding campaign, including defining your goals, setting a realistic budget, selecting a suitable crowdfunding platform, and creating a strategic marketing campaign?

Super Hack 29 | Who Wrote the Rule That Funding Has to Come with Giving Up Ownership of Your Company?
Steps and tips for raising capital without promising away your future earnings

"If everybody jumped off a cliff into a sea of sharks, would you do it, too?"

Maybe your parents posed a question like mine when you were young and easily influenced by what your friends were doing.

But what if your parents were wrong? What if following the crowd is the way to go?

When restaurateur and author of *Setting the Table*[12] Danny Meyer runs into a challenge or begins a new project, he asks questions starting with "Whoever wrote the rule…"

Entrepreneurs often do this intuitively – and spot opportunities no one else sees. But do you do it when you're finding funding? An excellent place to use this non-linear thinking is in funding your early-stage venture.

My question to you – which goes against my parent's "sea of sharks" logic – starts with Meyer's phrase:

"Who wrote the rule that funding has to come with giving up ownership of your company?"

Isn't that how companies have always attracted investors? By offering them ownership – and future money – in exchange for funding now?

However, that rule has some competition, and I'll use this space to share an alternative to traditional funding you may have yet to consider.

> Crowdfunding has altered the startup landscape by offering a unique way to secure funding, validate ideas, and build a community. By embracing this modern approach, you can tap into the power of the crowd, fostering a culture of innovation that benefits both creators and backers alike.

Quite simply, **crowdfunding**. In today's fast-paced digital age, crowdfunding has emerged as a powerful tool that allows entrepreneurs and innovators to bring ideas to life. By leveraging the collective power of the crowd, startups can secure financial support and gain access to a vast network of potential customers and investors.

The steps and tips for crowdfunding I provide below are general guidelines. Every entrepreneur and business is different, so figure out what path is most effective for you – whether it means using crowdfunding or not.

What is crowdfunding?

Crowdfunding is a collective effort to raise funds from many individuals, typically via online platforms, to support a specific project or venture. It provides a platform to present your ideas to a broad audience who can contribute varying amounts of money to the project.

These platforms act as intermediaries, connecting the project creators with potential backers. Crowdfunding campaigns often offer different tiers of rewards or benefits based on the contribution level, giving supporters an additional incentive to participate.

If you're searching for some platforms to begin your crowdfunding journey, here are some you might investigate: Crowdfunding Platforms for 2023.[13]

Benefits for startups.

Startups often need help securing traditional forms of financing, such as bank loans or venture capital funding. Keep in mind that this process has its pros and cons,[14] but crowdfunding does offer a range of advantages that make it an attractive option for many entrepreneurs:

- **Access to capital:** Crowdfunding enables startups to bypass traditional gatekeepers and tap into a broader pool of potential investors. This democratization of capital allows businesses to access funding from individuals genuinely interested in their product or concept.

- **Market validation:** Launching a crowdfunding campaign allows entrepreneurs to gauge market interest and validate their ideas. By presenting your project to the public, you can gather feedback, build a community of early adopters, and even secure pre-orders before going into production. This validation can be invaluable for attracting further investment and refining the product.

- **Marketing and exposure:** Crowdfunding campaigns generate significant buzz and media attention, giving you exposure you might not otherwise achieve. The social nature of these platforms encourages backers to share projects with their networks, expanding the campaign's reach and potentially attracting additional investors or customers.

The process of crowdfunding

According to Indeed writer Kelly Quinn, who has developed successful marketing strategies and managed national campaigns, the crowdfunding process typically involves the following steps.[15]

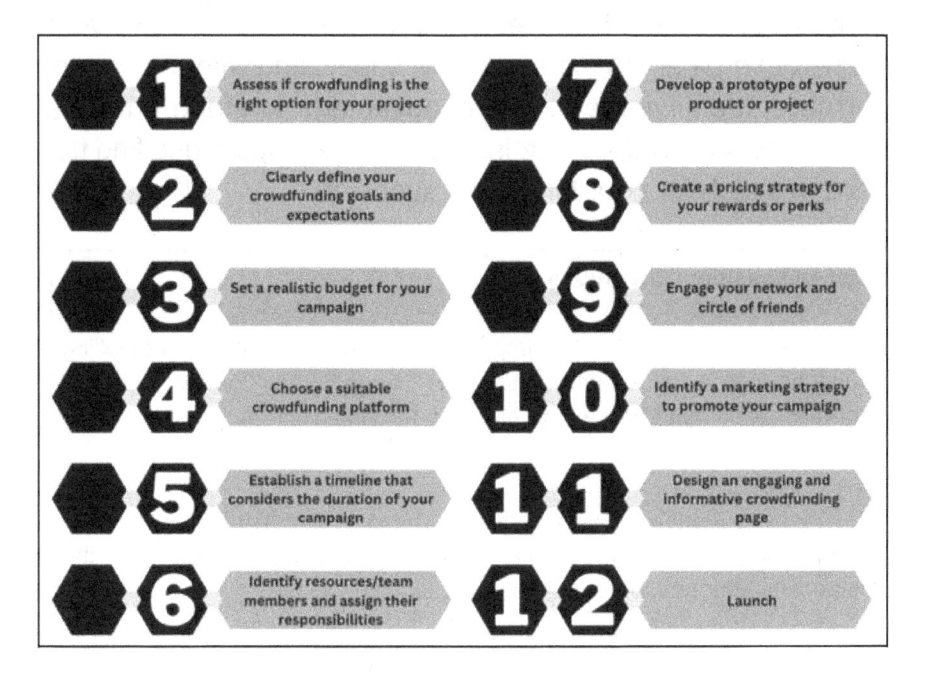

1. Assess if crowdfunding is the right option for your project
2. Clearly define your crowdfunding goals and expectations
3. Set a realistic budget for your campaign
4. Choose a suitable crowdfunding platform
5. Establish a timeline that considers the duration of your campaign
6. Identify resources/team members and assign their responsibilities
7. Develop a prototype of your product or project
8. Create a pricing strategy for your rewards or perks
9. Engage your network and circle of friends
10. Identify a marketing strategy to promote your campaign
11. Design an engaging and informative crowdfunding page
12. Launch

Traditional fundraising isn't lost here. The three F's – family, friends, and fools – who might have invested in the past are still essential to crowdfunding. You want them to be part of your crowd and to share your ask with their crowds, too.

The more, the merrier has never been a more accurate statement.

So, whether you're an aspiring entrepreneur or a passionate supporter of groundbreaking ideas, crowdfunding offers an exciting avenue to be part of the next big thing.

Which may or may not include a sea of sharks. Of course, Shark Tank is also an option.

Super Hack 30 | Pitch Like a Pro
Never underestimate – or under-develop – the power of your story

Beyond mere numbers and data, investors crave connection, purpose, and vision. Some essential elements can elevate your pitch from ordinary to extraordinary: captivating with a resonant narrative, identifying your unfair advantage to stand out from the competition, and evaluating investor participation to find the perfect match for your long-term success.

> **Self-Assessment Questions:**
>
> 1. Have you recognized the importance of incorporating a compelling narrative into your investor pitch that engages emotions and vividly portrays your entrepreneurial journey, mission, and the impact your venture aims to make?
>
> 2. Have you identified and clearly articulated your advantage and value proposition, demonstrating what sets your business apart from the competition through intensive market research?
>
> 3. Are you prepared to evaluate potential investors in terms of their financial contribution and based on their industry knowledge, track record, and connections that can bring added value to your venture, understanding there are trade-offs between autonomy and expertise to align with your long-term vision?

Super Hack 30 | Pitch Like a Pro
Never underestimate – or under-develop – the power of your story

"I came into this business the hard way," this biotech startup CEO told us. "It was a cancer diagnosis, a surprise cancer diagnosis, stage 4, metastatic cancer – and when I returned to my materials science lab, I knew I had zero tools to get at this problem."

That's how Dr. Greg Sawyer, founder of Aurita, started his investor pitch [16] captivating his audience with his personal story – before explaining what his company is trying to accomplish and why we should help him do so.

He started with a story – and it worked.

As an aspiring entrepreneur, one of the critical skills you must develop is the ability to deliver a compelling investor pitch .[17] It's not just about presenting numbers and facts; it's about captivating your audience with a story,[18] highlighting your competitive advantage, and understanding the value and benefits of investor ownership.

Let's explore these three key elements that can make your investor pitch a standout success.

Captivate with a narrative.

Behind every successful business lies a captivating story; weaving that narrative into your investor pitch can make all the difference. Investors are interested in more than just the numbers; they want to connect with the vision, passion, and purpose driving your venture.

Share the journey that led you to your business idea, the problems you aim to solve, and the impact you plan to make.

Shark Tank offers one "prescribed format." At the beginning of every pitch, business owners seeking investments begin by discussing their entrepreneurial journey and inspiration. The best ones have extraordinary storytelling abilities and confidence and are entertaining – people *want* to listen to them talk.

Aaron Krause, the inventor of Scrub Daddy,[19] gave an incredibly engaging pitch. Ultimately, he had the Sharks fighting over who would get to invest in what would become a huge success.

Identify your unfair advantage.

Knowing your unfair advantage[20] is crucial when delivering an investor pitch.

Investors seek to identify what sets your business apart from the competition.

> You can create a lasting impression by engaging their emotions and vividly portraying your mission. Remember, a compelling story can help investors see the potential beyond the figures and foster a genuine interest in your venture.

Clearly articulate your unfair advantage and value proposition. [21] You must explain why customers choose your product or service over others. Highlight any intellectual property, proprietary technology, strategic partnerships, or market differentiators that provide a sustainable edge.

Back To build credibility, back up your claims with market research, customer testimonials, or early traction. Additionally, it's crucial to deeply understand your target market,[22] , as your pitch must demonstrate your ability to sell effectively to this group. Instill confidence in investors and help them recognize the growth **potential of your venture.**

Evaluate investor participation – Not all investors are alike.

When seeking investment, it's essential to consider whether you are willing to give up some ownership in your company. While retaining complete control might be desirable, securing the right investors can provide invaluable expertise, networks, and resources that accelerate your business growth.

Evaluate the value that potential investors bring beyond the monetary aspect. Consider their industry knowledge, track record, and connections that can open doors to new opportunities.

Weigh the benefits against the potential loss of autonomy (are you ready to have a "boss"?) and find a balance that aligns with your long-term vision (do you have a plan to exit?). Remember, having the right investors on board can significantly increase your chances of success. All money is not equal or the same. The right investors offer more than just money.

As you build your pitch, you might want to check out Debi Kleiman's First Pitch [23] an excellent resource to help you develop your story. Pitching skills are not just for finding investors but for wooing clients, suppliers, and employees.

Remember, mastering the art of an investor pitch requires more than just financial projections. It includes a story (think about Debi's 4 H framework). Dr. Sawyer headed down the path of entrepreneurship because he sought a cure for what seemed a terminal disease.

I hope your story isn't as dramatic – but I'm sure it has a dose of reality. After all, it compelled you to get into this challenging, crazy thing called entrepreneurship.

By crafting an engaging story and highlighting the functionality of your business, you, too, can create a winning pitch that attracts the right partners and propels your venture toward success.

Super Hack 31 | Be a 'Purple Cow'
Be remarkable and master these 3 things to attract the "right type" of investors

Pay attention to crucial elements that make a venture investment-worthy, and focus on self-efficacy, team dynamics, and strategic planning. Drawing insights from psychology and real-world examples like Netflix, delve into the importance of belief in oneself, the power of a cohesive team, and the necessity of a well-structured business plan. By aligning these components, startups can enhance their investment worthiness and pave the way for a brighter future.

Self-Assessment Questions:

1. Do you genuinely believe in your ability to succeed in your venture and possess a growth mindset that views challenges as opportunities for learning and innovation? Are you emotionally agile and capable of managing self-doubt and discomfort associated with entrepreneurship?

2. Have you critically evaluated your team's composition, considering their relevant experience, expertise, and ability to work cohesively? Are your team dynamics strong, with a proven track record of effective communication, collaboration, and commitment to executing plans?

3. Does your business plan demonstrate rational upside potential by showcasing thorough market research, a clear understanding of target demographics, and a unique value proposition?

Super Hack 31 | Be a 'Purple Cow'
Be remarkable and master these 3 things to attract the "right type" of investors

Before Seth Godin wrote a book titled *The Purple Cow* [24] Sarasota, Florida, had its own. The Van Wezel Performing Arts Hall[25] remains a landmark on the edge of Sarasota Bay, with a roof shaped like a clamshell and inner and outer walls painted a distinctive purple.

The building opened in early 1970, and residents quickly dubbed it the "Purple Cow" and the "Purple People-Seater." But it drew performers such as Luciano Pavarotti, Lucille Ball, and Barry Manilow – and sold-out crowds – and still draws attention.

And that's "remarkable," according to Godin.

"Something remarkable is worth talking about. Worth noticing. It's interesting. It's a purple cow," he wrote in *The Purple Cow*. **"Boring stuff is invisible. It's a brown cow.** We've created a world where most products are invisible."

This is also true about startups raising outside investment.

When investing in a new venture, investors take time to consider before committing their resources.

Consider whether your venture is investment-worthy before you make the ask. That decision involves three key components: you, your team, and your plan.

Do you believe you can do it?

Both believing in your ability to succeed and having a solid growth mindset are pivotal in attracting investors.

Having those is what distinguished psychologist Albert Bandura termed "self-efficacy."

It is "the belief in one's capacity to complete a task, rather than the relevant skills possessed," Bandura said. It is the individual's internal confidence to influence events and control the environment to get stuff done no matter what.

It would be best to exhibit this confidence and resilience as the driving force behind your venture. It would be best if you viewed challenges as opportunities for learning and growth. You instill confidence in potential investors by showcasing your ability to adapt and overcome obstacles.

Furthermore, a growth mindset fosters innovation and encourages continuous improvement to the product or service, making it more appealing to investors seeking long-term growth prospects.

Perhaps a good way to measure this growth mindset is simply asking yourself what psychologist Susan David [26] asks: *"Are you agile?"*

Emotional agility, approaching inner emotional experiences in a mindful, values-driven, and productive way, is paramount to growth and innovation. It takes much courage to put everything at risk – money, reputation, family – and managing the self-doubt and second-guessing and everything else your mind and emotions throw your way are uncomfortable, too.

But, again, Susan David provides some words of wisdom: "Discomfort is the price of admission to a meaningful life."

Does your team – and each member of it – have what it takes?

Of course, you aren't going this path alone. Any venture's success relies heavily on your team's collective capabilities and expertise. Investors seek teams with diverse skill sets, complementary strengths, and a track record of achievement.

Additionally, investors are more likely to invest in teams demonstrating effective communication, collaboration, and a shared vision. The chances of securing investments significantly increase by showcasing strong team dynamics and a proven ability to meet commitments and execute plans consistently.

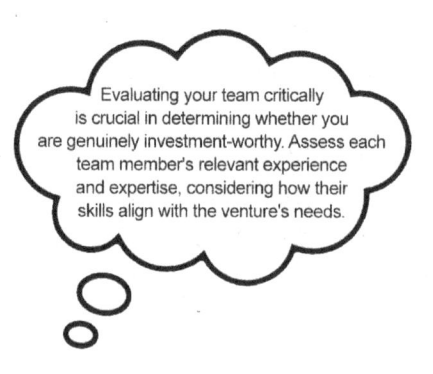

> Evaluating your team critically is crucial in determining whether you are genuinely investment-worthy. Assess each team member's relevant experience and expertise, considering how their skills align with the venture's needs.

Consider Netflix[27] and their team's evaluations. They consider how each employee contributes as part of their dream team – doing what is best for the company, not just the individual.

They model themselves as a professional sports team. Significant value is placed on their employees' abilities and what they bring. When evaluating your team, consider how they contribute and bring value to the company.

Does your plan demonstrate rational upside potential?

In addition to proving that you and your team are investment-worthy, you must demonstrate that your venture has significant upside potential to attract investors. Do you have the "purple cow" wow factor?

Conducting thorough research and planning is essential. Analyze the market landscape, identify target demographics, and assess competitors. Doing so gives you valuable insight into potential growth opportunities, market demand – and your unique, standout, one-of-a-kind selling points.

This research helps to develop a compelling business plan that showcases your remarkable company's clear path to profitability and scalability.

A well-structured plan demonstrates an understanding of the market and your ability to capitalize on emerging trends, making the venture more enticing to potential investors.

Demonstrating self-efficacy and a growth mindset instills confidence in investors while evaluating your team's skills and dynamics showcases your ability to execute plans efficiently.

Additionally, thorough research and planning help assess the potential of your venture and develop a compelling **and** realistic business plan. Practical planning means **no** hockey stick projections, Hail Marys, or ludicrous growth and market penetration assumptions.

Focusing on these aspects can enhance your investment worthiness, increasing the likelihood that you will attract the resources (know-how, money, customers, and talent) necessary to monetize the venture.

Purple paint is optional.

Super Hack 32 | Get Yourself Some Money
Prepare like an entrepreneur -- and an investor -- before you make the ask

Early-stage investing in startups can be tricky when examining the critical strategies entrepreneurs and investors need to navigate successfully. From setting appropriate funding rounds to executing robust business models and validating the market with paying customers, we explore the essential steps for investors and founding teams.

> **Self-Assessment Questions:**
>
> 1. Have you thoroughly evaluated and validated your business from an investor's perspective, considering appropriate pricing rounds, executing a winning business model, and securing early customers to demonstrate market demand?
>
> 2. Does your business model include a clear value proposition, scalable revenue generation plan, and a well-defined target market, setting the stage for sustainable growth and attracting potential investors?
>
> 3. Are you prepared to build a robust social capital network, raise funds in tranches based on milestones, and adapt contingency plans (Plan B, C, and D) to navigate the uncertainties and challenges of early-stage investing effectively?

Super Hack 32 | Get Yourself Some Money
Prepare like an entrepreneur -- and an investor -- before you make the ask

Early-stage investing in businesses holds excellent potential for both investors and entrepreneurs. However, navigating the complex landscape of startups requires a strategic approach to maximize returns and mitigate risks.

How can you secure adequate funding? Start by evaluating and validating your business and think like investors. What will they consider before offering you funding?

Price your rounds appropriately.

Let's say you score a spot on Shark Tank [28] How would you prepare for that?

You'll need to predetermine what your venture is worth, decide how much money you want to request and what percentage of your business you're willing to sacrifice.

Determining the right price for funding rounds is crucial for startups and investors. However, setting a valuation that accurately reflects your company's potential while maintaining investor interest is a delicate balancing act. Overvaluation can lead to inflated expectations, making future funding rounds challenging. Conversely, undervaluation may result in missed opportunities for growth and dilution of the founders' equity.

That means you must provide comprehensive financial data, market analysis, and a clear growth strategy to justify your valuation. Balancing realistic expectations with investor appetite ensures a healthy financial foundation for your business's future development.

Execute a winning business model.

An innovative and well-executed business model[29] is the backbone of any successful startup.

Investors seek startups with a clear value proposition and a scalable plan to generate revenue. You should identify a viable target market, understand customer needs, and differentiate yourself from competitors.

As you can see, developing a viable business model is more than a twenty-minute exercise.

Investors must assess the startup's business model for its ability to create sustainable growth. A robust business model considers revenue streams, cost structures, customer acquisition strategies, and scalability.

If you demonstrate a well-thought-out and adaptable plan, you'll have a higher chance of attracting investment and achieving long-term success.

Secure customers to validate your business.

Gaining early customers is crucial as it validates the market demand for your product or service. Investors are more inclined to back businesses with proven traction and a clear understanding of their customer base.

When evaluating a funding round, investors should consider your startup's growth trajectory, market potential, competitive landscape, inherent risks, and likelihood of achieving financial projections.

It would be best to build a robust customer acquisition and retention strategy to demonstrate your ability to generate revenue and scale.

Investors should assess a startup's customer acquisition metrics, such as customer lifetime value (CLTV) and customer acquisition cost[30] (Hint: (CAC). You should, too.) Startups showcasing a solid customer base and a strong product-market fit are more likely to attract follow-on investments and leverage their competitive edge.

In many instances, there is no better incentive for an investor than a paying customer.

Lots can go wrong, and often does.

As I reflect on many early-stage companies' fundraising successes and failures, capital-seeking companies should remember these tips.

1. **Your social capital network matters.** Networking and internet use allow you to form varied social – and often global – connections. Referrals matter. Be intentional about your choices.

2. **Raise funds in tranches.** Tranche investments let investors give you money over time instead of all at once. For instance, an investor might provide payments based on milestones you achieve. The more you deliver on your promises and de-risk the venture, the more likely funds will flow and follow.

3. **Be a contingency thinker.** Have a Plan B, C, and D. Recovery is essential to success. Things only go partially according to the forecast or plan.

4. **Look for funders aligned to your business temperament** and conducive to your business model.

Stage-appropriate investments are strategic, not opportunistic.

5. **Surround yourself with smart people who make you better**. This includes having a mentor to lean on as a sounding board and trusted advisor.

Early-stage investing requires careful consideration of various factors to ensure long-term success. Pricing rounds appropriately, executing a winning business model, and securing customers are essential pillars shaping your startup's future.

You can increase your chances of attracting investment and achieving sustainable growth. Simultaneously, investors can mitigate risks and improve returns by backing startups with solid financial foundations, scalable business models, and validated market demand.

These pillars lay the groundwork for a thriving startup ecosystem that fuels innovation and economic growth and creates economic prosperity.

That's how you can ensure you have what an investor wants – before you ask.

Super Hack 33 | Redefining Success on Your Terms
A shift in your mindset might be precisely what you need

Today's societal definition of success often revolves around wealth, status, and external validation, but what if we redefine it on our terms? Incorporate the transformative power of focusing on personal growth, fulfillment, and positive impact into your daily mindset and actions. By fostering a supportive network, maintaining a positive mindset, and cultivating a culture of care and positivity, we can redefine success according to our values.

> **Self-Assessment Questions:**
>
> 1. Have you shifted your mindset when defining success and realized the importance of self-efficacy – the belief in your ability to accomplish tasks and overcome obstacles?
>
> 2. Are you actively building a network of like-minded individuals who provide support, honest feedback, constructive criticism, and motivation to help you pursue your unique version of success?
>
> 3. Are you consciously harnessing positivity and maintaining high energy to drive personal growth, embrace new opportunities, and navigate challenges with optimism, all while redefining success on your terms rather than relying solely on traditional external markers?

Super Hack 33 | Redefining Success on Your Terms
A shift in your mindset might be precisely what you need

Success. It's a word that holds immense power and is often defined in our society as climbing the corporate ladder, amassing extreme wealth, or achieving societal recognition.

But what if we were to redefine success on our terms? What if we measured success through personal growth, fulfillment, and the positive difference and impacts we make?

Indeed, one way to redefine your success is by changing your mindset.

After Acquisition.com[31] co-founder Leila Hormozi[32] was jailed six times, she realized no one except herself was coming to save her. It was up to her to chart her path. So, she "brainwashed herself to success," she said, and went from jailbird to $100 million CEO.

This shift in mindset allowed her to plan precisely what she needed to do to achieve the vision of success she had in her mind.

And maybe that's what you should do, too.

It would be best if you believed you could do it yourself.

When redefining success, strong self-efficacy[33] is vital.

Self-efficacy refers to our belief in our ability to accomplish tasks and overcome obstacles. We become more resilient, driven, and willing to take risks when we possess a powerful sense of self-belief.

Through achievable goal setting, consistent challenges, and a shift in our focus from external validation to internal satisfaction, we can effectively redefine success for ourselves while reinforcing our belief in our capabilities.

With this as our foundation, we measure success through personal growth and progress rather than solely relying on external markers such as wealth, accumulated assets, or prestige.

Let others help you.

Creating a network of like-minded people who can offer proper support and honest feedback is critical. Surrounding oneself with positive, driven folks who share our beliefs and objectives fosters a growth-friendly environment.

Like-minded individuals don't just offer genuine support and honest feedback but also can aid through constructive criticism, refining your skills, and providing a fresh perspective.

Seeking individuals with these qualities will serve as a source of inspiration, motivation, and accountability, propelling us toward our unique version of success and helping us identify blind spots and avoid roadblocks that could impede growth.

Keep your energy high.

Redefining success relies on embracing positivity and maintaining energy to produce early wins.

We can tap into our full potential by harnessing our energy to cultivate a positive mindset. Plus, when our positivity fuels resilience and creativity, it helps us navigate challenges and setbacks from an optimistic point of view.

By creating momentum and gaining confidence in our abilities from the beginning, we can use these early experiences as stepping stones, reinforcing our belief in our version of success.

For businesses, maintaining this positivity from the beginning allows a company to remain consistently successful. CEO of KIND, Daniel Lubetzky,[34] describes the success that permeates his company because of fostering positivity.

"I love how the KIND family works together, with a commitment to each other and excellence. There's great energy across our team. You can feel it in the hallways of our office, and it inspires me to be better."

Another example of success is Delta's Care Fund [35] which provides employees with support services and resources to weather challenging situations such as a financial storm or a global pandemic.

In the depths of COVID, thousands of employees have been able to use the fund to address financial uncertainty. This benevolence shows Delta helps its people.

This shows that amazing things can arise when we take a vested interest in each other and surround it with a caring culture.

Success is unique to the individual and should not be confined to societal expectations or external measures alone. Redefining success on your terms requires a significant shift in perspective and a sharp

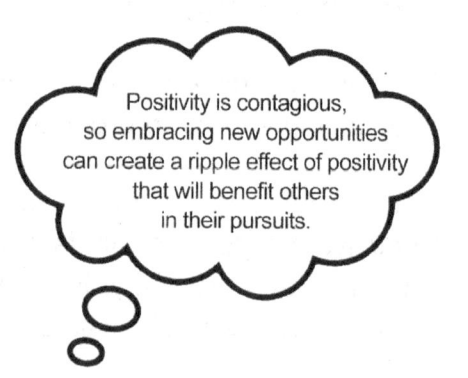

> Positivity is contagious, so embracing new opportunities can create a ripple effect of positivity that will benefit others in their pursuits.

focus on personal growth, fulfillment, and the positive impact we make.

By freeing ourselves from the limitations of traditional definitions of success, we can pave our path and create a life that aligns with our values, passions, and aspirations. Remember, true success lies in the journey, not just the destination.

Super Hack 34 | Stop and Smell the Roses
Foster meaningful connections
with others – and yourself

In today's whirlwind of responsibilities and ambitions, it's easy to lose sight of the value of meaningful connections and personal well-being. Remember the importance of stopping to appreciate the people around us and investing in our mental health. From prioritizing self-care activities to nurturing family relationships and maintaining a solid network, each aspect is vital to our happiness and success.

> **Self-Assessment Questions:**
>
> 1. Do you regularly prioritize self-care activities, such as exercise, meditation, or hobbies, to maintain good mental health and build a strong foundation for nurturing healthy relationships with others?
>
> 2. Are you actively investing time and effort in your work, family, and personal relationships, creating a positive and supportive environment at work, and fostering emotional well-being in your personal life?
>
> 3. Do you maintain a strong network of professional and personal connections by engaging in regular and meaningful interactions, staying in touch through various communication channels, and showing genuine interest in the well-being of others within your network?

Super Hack 34 | Stop and Smell the Roses
Foster meaningful connections with others – and yourself

In today's fast-paced world, getting caught up in the hustle and bustle of our daily lives is easy. However, amidst our busy schedules and professional ambitions, it is essential to remember the significance of cultivating and investing in our relationships.

The benefits of fostering meaningful connections and building community with others cannot be overstated.

It starts with you.

In the pursuit of success, many individuals tend to put their mental well-being on the back burner. However, maintaining good mental health is crucial for leading a fulfilling life and building strong relationships.

Taking time for <u>self-care activities</u> [36] such as exercise, meditation, and engaging in hobbies, can help alleviate stress and improve mental resilience. Additionally, seeking professional support when needed is a vital step toward self-care.

By prioritizing our mental health, we enhance our overall well-being and create a solid foundation for nurturing healthy relationships with others.

Appreciate your family.

Our work and personal families play distinct but equally significant roles. Cultivating and investing in these relationships can bring immense joy and support.

Fostering connections with colleagues and superiors can create a positive and collaborative environment in the workplace. Sharing ideas, helping, and celebrating each other's achievements builds a strong work family that enhances productivity and provides a network of support during challenging times.

Similarly, investing time and effort in our personal family relationships promotes emotional well-being and strengthens the bonds that define us. Regular family gatherings, open communication, and showing appreciation for one another's presence can create a sense of belonging and security.

Finding the perfect work-life balance[37] to be present at work and for your family can be difficult. It will rarely be 50-50. You must find the right balance that works for your life and satisfy both to the best of your abilities.

The best advice is to be productive and efficient while at work, then disconnect to spend time with your family and things that matter to you (biking, walking, reading, religious activities).

Maintain a strong network.

Maintaining a solid network is essential in both personal and professional spheres. To do so, it is crucial to foster regular and meaningful interactions.

Stay in touch through emails, phone calls, or social media platforms – sending a news article relevant to their work can go a long way. Engage in networking events, conferences, and industry gatherings to expand your circle and build new connections.

It's important to show *genuine* interest. Keeping an active presence and being reliable and trustworthy will help maintain and strengthen your network connections.

Cultivating and investing in our professional and personal relationships is an investment that yields priceless returns.

As we navigate through life, let us remember the immense power of relationships and dedicate time and effort to nurture them, for it is through these connections that we find fulfillment, support, and boundless possibilities.

Tips to keep in mind

- **It is more about your energy level than your time.** Evaluate things that deplete your energy or give you energy. Prioritize things that provide you with energy.

- **Find joy in saying "yes."** Say yes to activities that make you a better version of yourself or stretch your comfort zone whenever possible.

- **Carve out "me" time.** Don't procrastinate on achieving items on your "bucket list." Schedule these activities if a vacation to Greece, a yoga certification, or a trip to the beach with friends is on your list of things to do for yourself.

- **Block time out on your calendar.** The only way to prioritize you is to schedule it amidst the clutter and chaos of your Outlook. Be sure to block out time for specific "me" activities. If you want to write a book, carve out time on the schedule to do this work. If you want to learn ballroom dance, carve out "protected" time on the schedule.

- **Pay it forward.** Volunteer. Give back. Find ways to be generous. Donate your talent. Be kind to others and find a way to make a difference.

Super Hack 35 | Tips for Launching Your Venture
Aim for more exhilaration and fewer challenges with this advice

Embarking on a new venture demands careful planning and execution. Learn essential tips for a successful launch, starting with thorough market research and the concept of a Minimum Viable Product (MVP) to gather feedback. Understand strategic pricing strategies to balance value and profitability and emphasize the importance of establishing credibility and seeking mentorship. With informed decisions and strategic execution, you can navigate the challenges of launching a venture and thrive in a competitive market.

> **Self-Assessment Questions:**
>
> 1. Have you conducted thorough market research to understand customer preferences, market trends, and potential gaps in the market, and have you considered employing a Minimum Viable Product (MVP) to gather real-world feedback?
>
> 2. Are you pricing your product or service in a way that reflects its value, considering the benefits it brings to customers, unique selling points, and the competitive landscape?
>
> 3. Have you established credibility by demonstrating domain knowledge, building a robust online presence, and fostering relationships with industry influencers, and have you actively sought mentors, advisors, or consultants with industry experience to help you make informed decisions for your venture's success?

Super Hack 35 | Tips for Launching Your Venture
Aim for more exhilaration and fewer challenges with this advice

Embarking on a new venture can be an exhilarating journey, but it also comes with its fair share of challenges.

Whether you're a seasoned entrepreneur or a first-time business owner, careful planning and execution are crucial to launching your venture successfully.

What does the customer want? How will they perceive my product's value? How can I continue growing? Keep these questions in mind and consider my advice for launching your venture successfully.

Do your homework.

Before diving headfirst into your venture, conducting thorough market research is crucial. In fact, according to Bloomio CEO Max Lyadvinsky,[38] "The top reason for startup failure is **lack of market need**."

If nobody needs what you're selling – or you've mistargeted your audience – your venture is destined for failure.

Market research provides valuable insights into customer preferences, market trends, and potential gaps in the market that you can exploit. By understanding your target audience, their needs, and the competitive landscape, you can make informed decisions to increase your chances of success.

Furthermore, employ the concept of a Minimum Viable Product (MVP).[39] An MVP is a simplified version of your product or service that allows you to gather real-world feedback from early adopters.

It allows you to test the waters before investing significant time and resources. Many familiar companies, such as Uber and Dropbox, used this method when starting up.

Uber, for instance, made its UberCab app work only on iPhones or via SMS and was only available in San Francisco. It was enough to prove that the ride-sharing idea had a market at little risk or cost.

Dropbox's founders were even more conservative. Their MVP was a simple explainer video showing how Dropbox would work – before any service was built! The video garnered over 70,000 signups from people who wanted to know more – and let the founders know their product was wished to.

By using an MVP and iteratively refining your offering based on the feedback you gain, you can develop a product that meets customer demands while minimizing the risk of launching a product that doesn't resonate with the market.

A 2021 research study showed that a flawed business model and customer feedback triggered a tech startup to pivot the most.

Iterate on strategic pricing.

One common mistake a new venture makes is initially pricing products too low, believing it will attract more customers. While offering competitive pricing is essential, undervaluing your product can backfire by creating a perception of lower quality or undermining profitability.

Ash Maurya, a lean entrepreneur who runs a bootstrapped startup called Cloudfire, famously emphasized that pricing drives behavior. What behavior do you want to go for your

<u>product or service by pricing it this way? Reflect on some of his insights from running</u>[40] pricing experiments.

Instead, find a balance between pricing and perceived value. Consider the benefits your product or service brings to customers, the unique selling points, and the competitive landscape.

As you establish a strong position in the market and build a loyal customer base, you can gradually adjust pricing to reflect increasing brand equity.

You need more than money.

Launching a new venture requires more than just financial resources. Build credibility and surround yourself with like-minded individuals who can offer guidance, support, and expertise is vital. In a keynote talk at <u>today's NACCE conference</u>,[42] the speaker shared that one of his ingredients for recipe success was creativity over capital. Not that capital isn't important, but it is not the only thing needed for a venture to succeed.

Establishing credibility can be achieved through demonstrating domain knowledge, building a robust online presence, and fostering relationships with industry influencers.

Additionally, connecting with experts who can assist with risk mitigation and accelerate your venture's growth is crucial.

Seek mentors, advisors, or consultants who have experience in your industry and can help you navigate challenges, identify opportunities, and make informed decisions. Their guidance can significantly reduce the learning curve and increase your chances of success.

The research shows that effectively mentored startups survive longer, raise more outside funds, and grow revenues faster than non-mentored startups.

Launching a new venture is an exciting and challenging endeavor. Remember, the journey may be demanding, but with careful planning and execution, your experience has the potential to thrive in a competitive marketplace.

Super Hack 36 | Learn from Their Marketing Mistakes
3 cautionary tales warning of pitfalls you'll want to avoid

In the labyrinth of business, mistakes often illuminate the path to success, offering invaluable lessons for entrepreneurs and marketers alike. From legal compliance to customer retention and navigating controversial issues, each error presents an opportunity for growth and refinement. By studying these pitfalls, entrepreneurs can chart a course toward success with foresight and wisdom, avoiding costly blunders. Let us embrace the wisdom of learning from the past to forge a brighter future for our ventures.

> **Self-Assessment Questions:**
>
> 1. Have you prioritized legal compliance in your marketing strategies, ensuring that your campaigns adhere to all necessary permits and licenses to avoid potential fines, legal battles, and reputational damage?
>
> 2. Are you actively balancing efforts to attract new customers with nurturing relationships with your existing customer base, recognizing the importance of loyal customers as the lifeblood of your business?
>
> 3. Do you cautiously approach controversial social or political issues in your marketing, conducting thorough research and considering potential consequences to balance authenticity and avoid unnecessary controversy to maintain a positive brand image?

Super Hack 36 | Learn from Their Marketing Mistakes
3 cautionary tales warning of pitfalls you'll want to avoid

One of my colleagues is the youngest of five children – and she credits some of her success to her older siblings' failures. She had the benefit of seeing firsthand and learning from their mistakes; she didn't have to make those same missteps.

We, too, can benefit from the mistakes of other companies and leaders who have gone before us.

Because in the dynamic business world, failures and lessons learned often accompany success. Companies that have stumbled along the way usually can provide invaluable insights for entrepreneurs and marketers alike.

By examining their mistakes, we can avoid repeating them and pave a smoother path toward success.

Do things the right way... legally.

One of the crucial lessons we can learn from the market mistakes of other companies is the necessity of adhering to legal requirements before launching any unorthodox marketing campaign.

Time and again, businesses have found themselves in legal hot water because they needed to obtain the proper permits or licenses.

Whether it's an attention-grabbing stunt or a creative promotion, businesses must ensure they have the legal framework. Failure to do so can result in fines, legal battles, and reputational damage that can take years to recover.

In 2007, Cartoon Network [43] launched a guerrilla marketing campaign to promote one of their new movies. They placed a giant LED structure in Boston on support along Interstate 93, and a concerned passerby called 911 because this suspicious object had random wires sticking out. He thought it was a bomb.

It was a magnet that drew law enforcement and news agencies and, eventually, cost the head of Cartoon Network his job. If the company had gone through the proper channels, they could have avoided many headaches about their innocent advertisement.

Customer retention

Another essential lesson from market mistakes is the danger of losing touch with your core demographic. Companies that have fallen victim to this pitfall often prioritize chasing new markets and neglect their loyal customer base.

It's crucial to balance attracting new customers with nurturing existing relationships. Loyal customers are the lifeblood of any business, and losing their support can have devastating consequences.

Companies should invest in understanding their customers' evolving needs, preferences, and desires and adapt their marketing strategies accordingly.

In 2009, Radio Shack[44] tried to rebrand as "The Shack" to appeal to a younger demographic. They wanted to expand their target market but realized this did not have the effect they expected. The rebrand alienated their original target audience of loyal customers, causing them to lose valuable business.

In recent times, Delta's revamp of its SkyMiles programs likely cost it loyal customers, as it de-featured "perks," made Sky Club access more difficult, and made status harder for its most frequent and revenue-producing passengers. JetBlue and others took the opportunity to "status match" given Delta's missteps. While Delta backpedaled and added new benefits, tweaks, and other "loyalty" adjustments, it acknowledged irate customer responses by stating, "But your (loyal fliers) response made clear that the changes *did not fully reflect the loyalty you have demonstrated to Delta.*"

Cautiously approach controversial issues

Engaging with controversial social or political issues can be a double-edged sword in an era where social media amplifies every move a company or individual makes.

Numerous companies have faced backlash for taking a stance on polarizing topics that alienated a significant portion of their customer base. While businesses must align with their values and support social causes, caution must be exercised.

Consider recent issues facing Target, Bud Light, Disney, and others. Should corporations push activist agendas? In a world where we can't have civil discourse and lack respect for differing ideas, it seems increasingly risky for corporations and their leaders to speak on behalf of their brand without alienating some customers within the brand. More fundamentally, it can be highly detrimental when companies like AB InBev lose sight of who their Bud Light customers are. This sales fiasco and public relations crisis cost them more than $395 Million, and both sides of a controversial issue were left dissatisfied by the company's actions.

In 2015, Starbucks [45] CEO pushed a campaign to encourage people to discuss race. The company had baristas write "#race together" on coffee cups and discuss racial tension. This ultimately ended in disaster when critics felt it was not a coffee shop place to weigh in on racial issues.

"For example," one tweet stated, "I don't go to a mechanic for financial advice, and I don't take advice on race from my coffee. Sorry, Starbucks. #RaceTogether."

Just as my colleague learned from her siblings, learning from the market mistakes of other companies can save you from repeating costly blunders.

Entrepreneurs and marketers can navigate the business landscape more effectively by prioritizing legal compliance, staying connected with loyal customers, and cautiously approaching controversial issues.

Conduct thorough research and consider the potential consequences before taking a public stance on sensitive issues. Striking a balance between authenticity and avoiding unnecessary controversy is vital to maintaining a positive brand image.

Success comes not only from studying best practices but also from understanding the "best" pitfalls others have experienced and that we want to avoid. So, let us learn from the past to build a brighter and more promising future for our ventures.

Super Hack 37 | Growing Pains
3 mindsets for managing growth potential

The pursuit of growth is inherent to entrepreneurship, yet the path to expansion is fraught with challenges and pitfalls. There are many stories of entrepreneurs whose ambitious growth trajectory led to the downfall of their companies. These stories teach us the importance of balancing ambition with realism and the dangers of quickly scaling without sufficient preparation or capital.

Self-Assessment Questions:

1. How well do you assess the costs and timelines of expanding your business? Do you need to be more accurate regarding growth initiatives' financial and temporal requirements? Are you open to seeking advice from industry experts or experienced individuals to gain insights into the challenges and opportunities?

2. How do you approach the pace of growth for your company? Are you mindful of the risks associated with rapid expansion, such as straining resources, operations, and employee morale? Are you focused on achieving steady, controlled growth that aligns with your company's abilities?

3. How thoroughly is your market research and customer discovery approach when considering expansion opportunities? Do your research to understand new market dynamics, customer preferences, and competitive landscapes.

Super Hack 37 | Growing Pains
3 mindsets for managing growth potential

Entrepreneurs' ambition to expand and grow their businesses is a natural part of the startup journey. However, the allure of rapid expansion can sometimes lead to overlooking critical aspects of the process. While it's essential to seize opportunities, attempting to grow too fast can backfire.

Just ask Jim Picariello, [46] founder of Wise Acre Frozen Treats. Jim started his company in 2006, making organic popsicles from a schoolhouse kitchen. [47] It took him a year and a half to hire his first employee.

But six months later, he hired 14 more, moved to a larger manufacturing facility, and purchased expensive equipment when Wise Acre grew from filling orders of a few hundred dollars each for eight stores to an order for a national distributor that cost $45,000 worth of product.

It was precisely what he wanted –the death knell for his company.

By the end of 2008, Wise Acre had left the business, and Jim had to file for bankruptcy. His company had grown too big too fast, and he hadn't raised sufficient capital to back it up.

If we can learn anything from Jim's story, **think big, start small, and scale smart.**

So, how do you grow your company without putting it in jeopardy? I suggest these three things.

Be realistic.

One of the most prevalent mistakes when striving for rapid growth is underestimating the costs and timelines of expanding a business. It's easy to be overly optimistic, envisioning an immediate return on investment, but expansion often comes with unexpected expenses and delays.

Whether expanding physical locations, increasing production capacities, or entering new markets, each step demands careful planning and realistic growth targets.[48]

Otherwise, rapid growth becomes a pitfall.

Businesses must conduct meticulous research to identify potential hurdles and costs that might occur during the expansion process. Creating a detailed budget, considering various scenarios, and factoring in contingencies can help achieve a more realistic outlook.

Moreover, consulting with industry experts or seeking advice from those who have undergone similar expansions can provide invaluable insights into what to expect.

The author Jim Collins famously said, "Confront the brutal facts"[49] This means being realistic about your business goals and honest with yourself about expansion, eliminating or mitigating unknowns, and putting you on a focused path to success.

Go at your own pace.

While it might seem counterintuitive, growing too fast can harm a business. Rapid expansion can strain resources, operations, and employee morale. It can burn capital, churn employees, and dilute the customer experience.

When companies expand without solid foundations in place, it's akin to building a tower on a shaky base. Eventually, it will begin to crumble.

One of the most critical details in sustainable growth is maintaining the quality of products or services. If expansion compromises the standard, it can lead to dissatisfied customers and a tarnished reputation.

Moreover, a sudden increase in demand can lead to supply chain issues and fulfillment problems, resulting in disappointed clients, loss of clients, and missed opportunities.

It's essential to strengthen internal processes, ensure scalability, and invest in employee training and development. By aligning growth with the company's capacity, businesses can deliver a consistent and satisfactory customer experience while steadily expanding their operations.

Conduct adequate customer discovery (market research + customer validation).

The excitement of expansion can sometimes cloud a business owner's judgment, leading them to pay attention to proper market research.

Understanding the new market's dynamics, customer preferences, and competitors is vital for successful expansion. Without this information, a company may find itself entering a market in which there isn't enough demand for its goods or

> To tackle this demand issue, businesses should focus on smart growth - steady, controlled growth where quality, efficiency, and support systems are conducive to achieving the growth goals.

services or, worse, may find itself up against unanticipated intense competition.

<u>Conducting thorough market research</u>[50] allows businesses to identify opportunities, potential challenges, and the best approach to penetrate the new market. It helps craft a targeted marketing strategy and tailor products or services to meet the audience's needs.

While the ambition to grow a business is commendable and often desirable to compete and win, you must approach the journey cautiously and diligently, aligning the component pieces of the growth puzzle to win in the marketplace.

Underestimating expansion costs and timelines, expanding too quickly without proper preparation, and failing to conduct comprehensive market research are common pitfalls that hinder success.

By avoiding these obstacles and adopting a strategic approach, you can achieve sustainable growth and maximize your chances of long-term success.

Super Hack 38 | Growth Mode
3 triggers to profitably increasing revenue

Understanding that growth relies on customer-centricity and a skilled workforce, leverage your resources to incorporate both into your daily operations. Emphasize the importance of segmenting profitable customers and tailoring offerings to meet their evolving needs, challenging the status quo of customer acquisition-focused strategies. By embracing new strategies, businesses can face growth challenges and realize their long-term market objectives.

> **Self-Assessment Questions:**
>
> 1. How effectively do you prioritize customer segmentation and retention strategies to drive revenue growth in your business? Are you actively engaged in market research and customer feedback to understand evolving consumer needs and preferences?
>
> 2. How adept are you at recognizing untapped opportunities within your organization to drive growth? Do you regularly analyze your current customer base and purchasing patterns to identify cross-selling or upselling opportunities?
>
> 3. How effectively do you prioritize hiring and developing the right talent to support your business growth objectives? Are you focused on recruiting employees with unique skills and expertise?

Super Hack 38 | Growth Mode
3 triggers to profitably increasing revenue

In the dynamic business world, growth is the lifeblood that fuels success and propels organizations to new heights. While achieving sustainable business growth can be challenging, strategic planning and a forward-thinking approach can lead companies to success.

As you might expect, growing a company is all about the customer – and the team serving those customers – but today, I discuss different ways to think about both by providing three triggers that will lead to increased revenue.

Segment profitable customers.

At the heart of every successful business lies the ability to consistently increase sales and revenue while pursuing a profitable/optimum business mix. Companies must focus on both customer acquisition and retention strategies to achieve this.

Leveraging digital marketing tools and social media platforms can significantly boost your brand's visibility and attract a wider audience. Adopting an omnichannel approach[51] ensures a seamless customer experience, attracting new customers while fostering loyalty.

First, it is crucial to understand the target market and refine products or services to meet your existing customers' evolving needs. Conduct market research, seek customer feedback to gain valuable insight into consumer preferences, and tailor your offerings accordingly.

I have always found it frustrating that banks never focus on their existing customers. They are always on the hunt for new customers. They offer newcomers free services and extra cash but withhold perks from their current clients.

Banks aren't alone in this, of course. However, every strategy they undertake shows growth from recent customer acquisitions rather than better serving existing customers. I think that's a mistake.

Check the opportunities.

In the quest for business growth, it is essential to recognize the untapped potential that may already exist within your organization. Analyzing your current customer base and purchasing patterns can reveal opportunities to cross-sell or upsell products and services.

Introducing complementary offerings can lead to an increase in revenue without acquiring an entirely new customer base.

Disney and Delta do this exceptionally well. Delta offers highly differentiated multi-class services on the same plane and will now use hyper-segmentation to classify profitable flyers with their premium airport club lounges.

Disney is selling Genie + and Lightning Lanes. Some reports show that as many as 50% of park guests purchase Genie +, adding $1-3 million daily to park revenues with no increase in attendance. Today's significant shift is that customers will pay more for a highly differentiated customer experience.

Furthermore, exploring expansion opportunities[52] in new markets or geographic regions can open doors to fresh revenue streams. In-depth market research is crucial to understanding the demands and preferences of these potential customers.

Collaborating with local partners and adapting business strategies to suit regional nuances can give you a competitive advantage.

Find and select 'right fit' talent.

But above finding the right customers, you must find the right talent.

"Incredible things in the business world are never made by a single person but by a team," said Steve Jobs, co-founder of Apple.

As businesses grow, so do their demands for specialized skills and expertise. Hiring the right employees[53] with the unique talents your business needs can foster innovation, creativity, and problem-solving capabilities within the organization.

Investing in employee training and development is equally important. By providing opportunities for upskilling and continuous learning, companies can nurture a workforce equipped to handle new challenges and responsibilities with business expansion.

Additionally, offering competitive compensation packages, perks, and employee benefits can aid in attracting top talent and retaining valuable team members. The best organizations select talent; they don't hire employees; the Disney Institute has hammered this truth into my head.

I want to be the best organization – and I want my choice of talent. Don't you? Indeed, sustainable business growth requires a strategic and multifaceted approach. Adaptability, innovation, and a customer-centric approach will guide your journey toward success and prosperity.

Embracing these strategies will enable you to thrive in an ever-evolving marketplace and achieve your long-term objectives. Segmenting your customers and finding innovative ways to upsell and cross-sell – with the right talent in place – will provide a more sustainable revenue stream to meet your stretch goals.

Super Hack 39 | Throw in the Towel
3 skills for bouncing back

We confront one of the most daunting decisions for entrepreneurs: knowing when to walk away from a business idea. While passion and determination are essential, they must be balanced with objective analysis. Drawing inspiration from the experiences of industry titans like Bill Gates, who turned failure into motivation for success, we explore three critical factors to guide this pivotal decision-making process. By embracing failure as a learning opportunity, entrepreneurs can remain resilient.

Self-Assessment Questions:

1. How effectively have you embraced the concept of "failing fast and smart" in your entrepreneurial journey? Have you been proactive in testing, gathering feedback, and learning from setbacks to pivot when necessary?

2. Can you objectively evaluate the potential success of your business idea or project, or are you letting emotions cloud your judgment? How consistently do you step back to make decisions based on actual data rather than emotional attachment?

3. Have you actively sought and engaged with trusted advisors and stakeholders to gain diverse insights on your venture? How open are you to constructive criticism, and how effectively do you use it to identify weaknesses and explore new approaches?

Super Hack 39 | Throw in the Towel
3 skills for bouncing back

One of the most challenging decisions an aspiring business owner or project leader can face is determining when to quit. When is it time to let go of an idea or a venture? While you need passion and determination to drive you toward success, they aren't enough.

You need a viable project.

In this hack, we will explore three crucial factors to guide you in recognizing when to stop pursuing a business idea or project.

Even the brightest minds sometimes call it quits. In the '70s, Bill Gates started his first business --Traf-O-Data.[54] It was an exciting beginning of his entrepreneurial journey, but sadly, the excitement didn't last long.

Traf-O-Data was a failure, but one that taught Gates valuable lessons. He took the skills and experience from this venture to create the successful company we're all familiar with – Microsoft.

Fail fast and smart.

"Fail fast and fail forward."[55] It might sound counterintuitive, but failing can be integral to the entrepreneurial journey. The key is to fail faster and smarter. The innovation flywheel. Iterate. Learn. Unlearn. Experiment. Launch. Pivot. Repeat the cycle.

This means rapidly testing your assumptions, hypotheses, and prototypes in the real world while gathering feedback and learning from each setback. This allows you to identify potential flaws or unmet market needs early on, saving you from wasting valuable time and resources on a project that may not be viable.

By embracing failure as a natural part of the process, you can remain open to constructive criticism and pivot when necessary. The goal is not to avoid failure at all costs but to fail strategically, using the insights gained to make informed decisions about the future of your venture.

Setbacks are par for the course. You cannot master the entrepreneurial journey without a few mulligans.

Be logical.

Entrepreneurs often invest significant money, time, energy, and emotional attachment to their ideas or projects. Consequently, emotions can cloud judgment,[56] making it challenging to objectively evaluate the potential for success. To overcome this hurdle, stepping back and making decisions based on rational analysis rather than emotional attachment is crucial.

Start by thoroughly assessing your business idea. Then, consider market research, customer feedback, financial projections, and competitor analysis while developing clear criteria for success and setting specific milestones to gauge progress. Regularly revisit these criteria and be honest about whether the project meets expectations.

Seek advice.

Entrepreneurship can be a solitary journey, but that doesn't mean you must make every decision alone.

Engage with trusted advisors and stakeholders to gain valuable insights

> Please be open to feedback when seeking advice, even if it challenges your initial beliefs. Constructive criticism can help you identify weaknesses in your business idea and explore alternative approaches.

and wisdom. These individuals can be mentors, experienced entrepreneurs, industry experts, or potential customers, and their diverse perspectives can illuminate blind spots and potential opportunities you might have missed.

Any entrepreneur must know when to stop pursuing a business idea or project. You must learn to handle this challenging aspect of entrepreneurship, embracing the learning process and remembering that every setback is another opportunity for growth and progress in your entrepreneurial journey.

Most entrepreneurs have more than one good idea. Their first idea is seldom their best. Don't be defeated by setbacks. Mishaps. Do-overs and pivots. You find venture success only through iteration, experimentation, and gaining insights, but when you do, the price of admission is well worth the journey.

Super Hack 40 | Goal Setting
Stick to these three fundamentals to attain your aspiration

The concept of goal setting may seem straightforward; however, it requires a nuanced approach to ensure effectiveness. By balancing ambition and reality, breaking big dreams into manageable steps, and prioritizing self-care and collaboration, entrepreneurs can embark on a consistent growth and achievement journey.

Self-Assessment Questions:

1. Do you ensure goals are realistic and attainable given the current resources available to your team? How do you balance ambition with practicality to avoid frustration and encourage stable growth?

2. How effectively do you break down big dreams into smaller steps to make progress towards achieving them? Can you maintain motivation by celebrating small wins and staying focused on the end goal rather than getting overwhelmed?

3. Do you recognize and respect your limits when pursuing your goals, prioritizing self-care, relaxation, and maintaining a healthy work-life balance? How do you leverage teamwork, delegation, and collaboration to prevent burnout?

Super Hack 40 | Goal Setting
Stick to these three fundamentals to attain your aspiration

One of the best ways to achieve personal growth is by <u>setting goals</u>.[60] Not only does this push you in the right direction, but it can also help fulfill your sense of purpose.

When doing so, it's vital to keep the fundamentals in mind. That means making realistic goals, breaking big dreams into smaller steps, and knowing your limits.

Produce realistic results.

A common mistake when setting goals is aiming too high without considering your company's current abilities and resources. While aspiring for greatness is admirable, setting unattainable goals for your team can lead to frustration and discouragement among employees.

<u>Realistic goal setting</u>[61] is figuring out the path that best ensures each worker achieves sustainable, measured growth. It involves assessing your strengths, weaknesses, and the resources available to you *before* outlining your team's goals.

Understand your limitations and remember that growth takes time, discipline, and focus.

Imagine your dream of starting your own business. You might begin by setting simple milestones such as researching the market, drafting a business plan, or learning the basics of entrepreneurship. These stepping stones will keep you motivated and help you gradually build the skills and knowledge you need to achieve your goals.

However, completing a to-do list doesn't equate to producing results. Be intentional with your work and focus on the end goal rather than trying to do the most. As my first boss told me on my first day of work, "results, not effort, get rewarded."

Dream big, start small, scale fast.

Dreaming big[62] is a crucial driver of success. It pushes you out of your comfort zone and encourages you to aim for the extraordinary.

While it will help you identify your larger goal, you must complete a roadmap of smaller tasks to achieve it. Progress might seem slow sometimes, but remember that each small step brings you closer to your grand vision.

Suppose you're passionate about writing a novel. Instead of fixating on the finished manuscript, break down the process. Start by outlining the plot, developing characters, and setting a daily word count goal.

Celebrate each completed chapter or milestone, as these small wins will sustain your enthusiasm.

Tackling these small steps will also help you gain momentum and scale faster.

Know your limits.

Driving yourself to burnout is a common problem when pursuing your goals, as it's easy to get caught up in the excitement of building your own business. However, you can avoid this trap through planning.

This includes crafting a schedule that allocates time for your goal-related tasks, relaxation, self-care, and spending time with loved ones. Overexertion results in diminished returns, while a well-rested mind is creative, focused, and resilient.

> Setting practical goals is a delicate balance between your ambition and reality. However, by making them realistic, breaking down big dreams into small steps, and knowing your limits, you can pave the way for consistent growth without the risk of burnout.

Another great way to prevent burnout is through teamwork and collaboration. Rarely does a single individual possess all the talents needed to be an entrepreneurial success. Ensure you surround yourself with a diverse and talented team to help you navigate the challenges, obstacles, and setbacks you'll encounter along your journey.

Surround yourself with people who bring out the best in you, and you'll soon find your goals aren't so far out of reach after all.

After taking your first step, focus on building habits and a solid routine to keep achieving those goals.

It takes time, but elevating your mindset to higher levels of personal and professional growth is well worth it.

Super Hack 41 | Switch it Up
Strategies to Better Results

From embracing a proactive mindset to fostering cross-functional collaboration and mastering the art of saying "no," these strategies are crucial for achieving sustained growth and success. By adopting stronger approaches to problem-solving, nurturing collaborative relationships within teams, and strategically managing time and energy, entrepreneurs can overcome challenges to propel their ventures forward efficiently.

Self-Assessment Questions:

1. How effectively do you embrace the concept of "hustle" in your entrepreneurial endeavors? Are you proactively identifying and addressing potential challenges before they escalate?

2. What strategies do you have to promote employee interactions and cultivate a culture of cross-functional collaboration within your organization? How do you ensure that team members understand the interconnectedness of different departments and overarching business goals?

3. How do you approach the response of saying "no" strategically when it comes to meeting invitations and other demands on your time as an entrepreneur? How do you prioritize meetings and activities that align with your current objectives?

Super Hack 41 | Switch it Up
Strategies to Better Results

As a business-building entrepreneur, navigating the complex business world requires strategic thinking, innovative ideas, and the right mindset. Your approach to challenges, interactions with employees, and time management can significantly impact the success of your venture.

Let's delve into three crucial strategies to avoid and change as an entrepreneur.

Embrace hustle.

One of the most detrimental mindsets an entrepreneur can adopt is constantly being in "firefighting" mode. Reacting to problems as they arise rather than preventing them can lead to a chaotic and inefficient business environment. The most humble and agile entrepreneurs are contingent thinkers. They see around corners and have a plan A, B, and C.

Instead, entrepreneurs should strive to identify and address potential issues before they escalate proactively. You create a more stable and sustainable business by anticipating challenges and crafting strategies to mitigate them.

Smart and savvy entrepreneurs allocate time for regular evaluations of their processes, products, and services. This approach prevents potential crises and paves the way for continuous improvement.

Embracing a proactive mindset allows you to channel your energy into long-term growth and innovation rather than merely putting out fires.

As my friends and colleagues Dr. Matt Marvel and Dr. Kuratko opined, "Entrepreneurial hustle leads to venture performance and willingness to invest because urgent behaviors allow individuals to advance their goals, and **unorthodox behaviors** allow entrepreneurs to be more innovative."

Look at these seven unorthodox behaviors[63] ranging from quietly reading business memos at the start of a meeting to a doodling notebook for sketches and big business ideas. Which do you identify most with? Least?

Nurture "intensive" employee interactions.

Entrepreneurs often wear multiple hats, and it's easy to get lost in the minutiae of daily tasks. However, overlooking the importance of helping employees understand how their work contributes to other departments and the business can hinder growth.

Encouraging a siloed mindset among your team members can lead to miscommunication, duplication of efforts, and decreased morale.

To counter this, cultivate a culture of cross-functional collaboration[64] and holistic understanding. Regularly communicate the interconnectedness of different departments and demonstrate how each team's contributions align with the overarching business goals.

When employees see the bigger picture, they are more likely to take ownership of their roles and work harmoniously with others, ultimately driving efficiency and innovation throughout the organization. Gallup's Strength of the Workplace reminds me of one of the most important Q12 engagement questions,

"Do you have a best friend at work?" Those that do are likely to be more engaged and connected to their work and each other.

Serendipitous collisions and impromptu exchanges are foundational to the innovation process. They rarely happen in isolation or alone in your basement or extra room.

Just say "no."

Entrepreneurs often find themselves inundated with meetings that eat into their precious time. While meetings are essential for communication and decision-making, saying "yes" to every invite can drain your productivity and divert your focus from critical tasks. A key mindset to avoid is the belief that attending every meeting is necessary.

While extraordinary customer experiences are built on saying yes as much as possible, entrepreneurs must protect and conserve their energy for the most important "move the needle" activities. Time is energy. Entrepreneurs need to protect theirs.

Shark Tank's Mark Cuban[65] protects his time and energy by saying "no" to some meetings. He believes the biggest time waster is attending a meeting that doesn't make him money. While we all don't have the luxury of applying this litmus test exclusively, it reinforces the notion of protecting your time.

By mastering the art of discernment, you can allocate your time more effectively and dedicate your energy to high-impact activities that drive your venture forward.

> Learning to say "no" strategically can be a powerful tool. Prioritize meetings that align with your current objectives and directly impact your business. Politely decline invitations to gatherings that don't contribute significantly to your goals or can be addressed through other means of communication.

Your mindset plays a pivotal role in shaping the trajectory of your business.

By being more strategic and intentional – embracing hustle, nurturing collaboration, and saying "no" more often, you can create a more proactive and harmonious work environment and pave the way for sustained growth and success in your entrepreneurial journey.

Super Hack 42 | The Art of Self-Sabotage
3 roadblocks you must avoid on your path to entrepreneurial success

Self-sabotage, a phenomenon deeply rooted in human psychology, can pose significant challenges to business success. From insufficient funds to imposter syndrome and the misconception of "exhausted" innovation, these roadblocks can derail entrepreneurial dreams before they even begin. However, recognizing these obstacles is crucial for achieving lasting success. By challenging limiting beliefs, seeking guidance, and embracing creativity and adaptability, entrepreneurs can overcome these barriers.

> **Self-Assessment Questions:**
>
> 1. Have you fallen into the trap of believing that insufficient funds are holding you back from starting your entrepreneurial journey? Have you brainstormed more untraditional methods of raising funds and receiving investments?
>
> 2. Do you often experience imposter syndrome, feeling like you lack the knowledge or competencies needed to succeed in entrepreneurship? Are you intentional about how you adapt, seek guidance, and make progress toward your goals, regardless of any uncertainties you may face?
>
> 3. Are you hindered by the misconception that all the good ideas in your industry have already been claimed, leading to a sense of "exhausted" innovation? How can you break free from this limiting mindset by approaching business ideas from unique angles, combining existing concepts in new ways, or catering to underserved niches?

Super Hack 42 | The Art of Self-Sabotage
3 roadblocks you must avoid on your path to entrepreneurial success

In the mythology of entrepreneurship, we often grapple with internal barriers that can prove more detrimental than external challenges. The phenomenon of self-sabotage, particularly regarding business success, is a fascinating yet disheartening aspect of human psychology.

Don't let it stop you. You will encounter infinite problems between you and success, but remember that you **can** sidestep the danger and find a solution.

These are some roadblocks you might encounter on your entrepreneurial journey.

Insufficient funds

Too often, aspiring entrepreneurs are held hostage because they lack the financial resources to launch their dream venture. The illusion of needing a substantial sum upfront can act as a paralyzing force, preventing them from even taking the first step.

Is this you?

Many successful businesses start with minimal funding. The digital connectivity age has ushered in many cost-effective opportunities for launching and marketing a business.

You can establish a significant online presence without a hefty investment, from building a basic website to utilizing social media platforms. You can seek out investors, do crowdfunding, or start small with bootstrapping[66] — all are viable paths to sidestep this self-imposed financial blockade.

Imposter syndrome

Another common mental hurdle many entrepreneurs face is needing to be more knowledgeable or have more significant business competencies to succeed. This imposter syndrome[67] can be particularly debilitating, eroding your confidence and decision-making abilities.

The truth is that no one starts with all the answers. Every entrepreneur embarks on their journey with a degree of uncertainty.

What separates successful entrepreneurs from those who succumb to self-sabotage is their willingness to learn, adapt, and seek guidance—recognizing that every setback is an opportunity for growth. This is often where place-based entrepreneurship programs like business incubators can make the most difference – adding credibility, clout, and confidence to the business builders served through the program.

'Exhausted' innovation

A pervasive misconception that stifles budding entrepreneurs is the belief that all the good ideas have already been claimed. This mindset undermines creativity and innovation,[68] leading to a self-fulfilling prophecy in which potential breakthroughs remain undiscovered.

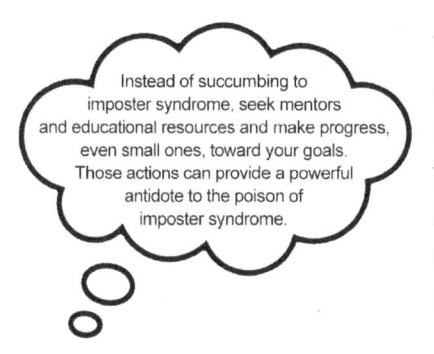

> *Instead of succumbing to imposter syndrome, seek mentors and educational resources and make progress, even small ones, toward your goals. Those actions can provide a powerful antidote to the poison of imposter syndrome.*

The world constantly evolves, and new problems arise, requiring novel solutions. Break free from the crippling mindset of "exhausted" innovation and approach business ideas from unique angles, combining existing concepts in new ways, or catering to underserved niches.

The success of businesses such as Airbnb, Uber, and even modern food delivery services demonstrates that you can birth revolutionary ideas in seemingly saturated markets.

Be sure the road to your business success will be paved with internal and external challenges. However, remember this: we often place the most insidious roadblocks in our way. Don't let a lack of money or the belief that you aren't qualified stop you. I don't think all the best ideas have already been claimed.

Those are patterns of self-sabotage. Recognize them, then actively counter them with determination, adaptability, and a healthy dose of self-belief. Aspiring entrepreneurs – that includes you! – can unleash their true potential and embark on a journey toward lasting success.

Super Hack 43 | Discovering Your "Why"
3 reasons for purpose-building your company

Your "why" is more than just a financial goal; it's the driving force behind your entrepreneurial journey, pushing you through challenges and defining your impact on the world. Whether it's empowering underprivileged communities, promoting sustainability, or revolutionizing technology, your mission should reflect your genuine interests and beliefs. By intertwining your mission with your business, you not only find joy and fulfillment in your work but also contribute to positive change in society.

> **Self-Assessment Questions:**
>
> 1. Have you taken the time to introspect and identify what truly fuels your passion in business? How does your mission align with your values and beliefs?
>
> 2. When considering your entrepreneurial ventures, do you ensure that your chosen business aligns with your "why" and allows you to channel your passion into actionable results? How do you intertwine your mission with your business to find joy, excitement, and fulfillment in your work?
>
> 3. In what ways does your business contribute to the greater good beyond personal ambitions and profit? How do you integrate social or environmental responsibility into your business practices to attract like-minded customers and create a positive impact on society?

Super Hack 43 | Discovering Your "Why"
3 reasons for purpose-building your company

Eighty-one percent of all entrepreneurs[69] create a business by choice instead of necessity. Freedom and passion,[70] not money, are the main motivations behind launching a company.

Being your own boss, starting something from the ground up, and growing and building something of your own for the long term are solid motivations for launching and staying with your venture – even in adversity or wide fluctuations with no feeling of near-term success.

In the ever-evolving landscape of business, finding your "why" is not just a philosophical pursuit – it's a crucial step toward creating a fulfilling and successful company.

Your "why" is your purpose, the driving force, the core reason behind your business endeavors. It gets you out of bed each morning, propels you through challenges, and ultimately defines your impact on the world.

Let's uncover your "why" in business.

A mission that ignites passion.

Discovering your "why" starts with introspection. What truly fuels your passion? [71] What issue, cause, or goal resonates deeply with you?

Your mission should be more than just a financial goal; it should align with your values and make you excited to dedicate your time and

> By intertwining your mission with your business, you find joy, excitement, and fulfillment in your work and become a more authentic advocate for your cause and advancing your vision.

energy. Whether empowering underprivileged communities, promoting sustainable practices, or revolutionizing technology, your mission should reflect your genuine interests and beliefs.

When your work is driven by passion, it becomes less about the challenges and more about the journey toward making a meaningful societal and community impact.

A business that excites you.

Choosing the right type of business is pivotal in aligning with your "why." Entrepreneurs often find themselves caught in the allure of compelling opportunities, only to realize that the need for more and connection to the business hinders their traction and growth.

Your business should be a vehicle to carry out your mission, allowing you to channel your passion into actionable results.

If you're an environmental enthusiast, a sustainable fashion brand might be your ideal avenue. If technology innovation is your calling, a startup focused on cutting-edge solutions could be the path for you.

Contribute to the greater good.

The most powerful "why" often transcends personal ambitions and extends to the greater good. How can your business positively impact society?[72] What change can you drive that goes beyond your bottom line?

Today's consumers are drawn to brands with a purpose beyond profit, and this trend is only growing stronger. By intertwining your mission with a commitment to social or environmental betterment, you attract like-minded customers and contribute to positive change.

Whether it's through charitable initiatives, ethical sourcing, or community engagement, your efforts can ripple out and create a more meaningful and dramatic impact. You can actualize your potential and passion through intentional and focused efforts.

Finally, finding your "why" in business is a multifaceted journey that involves aligning your passion, business, and impact with your greater good. It's about creating a symbiotic relationship and aligning your values, aspirations, and professional pursuits.

When you identify a mission that ignites your passion, a business that excites you, and a way to contribute positively to society, you're on the path to building not only a successful enterprise but also a profoundly fulfilling and purpose-driven life as an entrepreneur.

So, embark on this journey of self-discovery, and let your "why" guide you toward success, growing your significance and leaving an enduring and powerful legacy. Nothing is more satisfying than leaving things better than you found or starting a movement more significant than you – as the lyrics reinforce, the sky's the limit.

Super Hack 44 | The Power of Perseverance
3 mindsets for fulfilling our goals

Perseverance, often equated with stick-to-itiveness, isn't just about enduring hardships; it's about staying aligned with purpose despite the obstacles that come our way. Learn how to cultivate this vital trait, starting with finding purpose — a deeply personal value that fuels our actions and motivations. Emphasize the importance of celebrating wins, no matter how small, and leveraging failures as opportunities for growth and learning. Maintaining a growth mindset is the most essential, as it enables us to view setbacks as opportunities.

> **Self-Assessment Questions:**
>
> 1. How well-aligned are your personal goals and actions with your sense of purpose? What steps can you take to strengthen this alignment and enhance your inner strength?
>
> 2. How do you currently approach failures and setbacks in your journey towards achieving your goals? Do you see them as opportunities for growth, or do they tend to discourage you?
>
> 3. What strategies can you implement to foster a more resilient and growth-oriented mindset? How can you cultivate a mindset that views failures as valuable learning experiences to improve future actions?

Super Hack 44 | The Power of Perseverance
3 mindsets for fulfilling our goals

In life's journey, one trait stands out as a true game-changer: <u>perseverance</u>. [73] It's the steadfast commitment to keep going, even when the path seems rocky and the odds insurmountable.

Stick-to-itiveness, another way to think of perseverance, is a determination to keep going despite adversity. It is an entrepreneur's best friend, the driving force behind achieving goals and fulfilling dreams.

If you want perseverance, you must become your support system. Here's how.

Find your purpose.

Life's challenges become more manageable with a clear sense of <u>purpose.</u> [74] I don't mean the purpose of your company. I mean *your* purpose. Yes, I'm getting personal.

<u>American author and life coach Tony Robbins</u>[75] suggests purpose drives us to be our absolute best, and he provides some self-reflective questions to help you find yours: "How will you give back to the world? Looking back on your life, what will be your biggest accomplishment? Your biggest regret?"

That reflection will help you find your purpose – and your inner strength. Robbins describes inner strength as "a deep, unstoppable belief in yourself."

Perhaps a perseverance in believing you can do, be, or become?

Perseverance isn't merely enduring hardships but staying true to your purpose despite obstacles.

I'd recommend you check out your degree of personal alignment with this <u>wheel of life assessment</u>.[76] By closely looking at your alignment, you can intentionally close the gap between where you are and where you want to be.

Celebrate wins and "power" through failures.

Perseverance isn't just about forging ahead; it's also about knowing when to celebrate. Celebrating your wins, no matter how small, is crucial for maintaining your motivation. It reinforces that your efforts are paying off and that you're on the right track.

However, failures are inevitable. They can be disheartening, causing some to abandon their pursuits altogether. But a true champion sees failures as opportunities for growth. Instead of letting failure define them, they use it as a stepping stone to success. Every setback is a chance to learn, adapt, and get closer to their goals.

It depends on how you see failure. Intellectually curious people are vulnerable, impulsive, and easily distracted – but they're also open to making mistakes and having false starts.

They see failure as lessons on their path to success, not their downfall.

I'm not suggesting you fail on purpose. While failure isn't a scarlet letter, it isn't a badge of honor either. Failure carries both societal and real consequences. You might lose your outside investors' money. You might lose talented employees or an important customer.

Don't let failure define you or dictate the terms to you. Failure isn't career-limiting. It is career-enhancing. One of my colleagues – a professor and coauthor, <u>Dr. John Danner – opined</u>,[77] "Not only should we acknowledge the existence of failure, but we should treat it as a resource on par with an organization's other resources – financial, technological, and human resources." I love his notion that "failure is grief but not game over." Somehow, that sentiment provides me an enormous amount of relief when deep in innovation's complexities, chaos, and uncertainties.

Maintain a strong mindset.

Perseverance and a growth mindset go hand in hand. A growth mindset[78] is the belief that abilities and intelligence can be developed through dedication and hard work. When you approach challenges with a growth mindset, you're more likely to persevere because you view setbacks as temporary and opportunities for improvement.[79]

The good news is that we can change our mindset – with habit-forming activities, a positive attitude, and an outside support system.

Imagine someone starting a business. They may encounter financial difficulties, competition, and unexpected setbacks.

With a growth mindset, they'll see these challenges as chances to learn and innovate. They won't be discouraged by initial failures; instead, they'll adapt their strategy and keep pushing forward.

Perseverance is the unwavering determination to overcome obstacles and achieve your goals. Stay true to your purpose and learn to grow through wins and losses. Maintain a growth mindset despite setbacks.

By embodying these principles, you can navigate life's challenges gracefully and thrive. In short, when faced with adversity, persevere.

Super Hack 45 | The KonMari Method
3 ways to declutter your business life

In the pursuit of success, our lives and businesses often become cluttered with unnecessary tasks, projects, and distractions. However, what if the key to unlocking productivity and fulfillment lies in decluttering? Enter the KonMari Method, a revolutionary approach to tidying up created by Marie Kondo. By applying these principles to your business practices, you can streamline operations, focus on what truly matters, and eliminate anything that no longer serves your goals.

> **Self-Assessment Questions:**
>
> 1. Are there any projects or tasks that no longer align with your company's mission or goals? How can you apply the KonMari Method to declutter your business practices and focus on what truly matters?
>
> 2. Do you find yourself getting stuck in endless planning cycles, or do you prioritize taking action? How can you shift from overthinking to a bias for action, following the principles of the KonMari Method?
>
> 3. Do you and your team feel delighted with the work you're doing? How can you cultivate a work culture that promotes joy and satisfaction, leading to increased productivity and success?

Super Hack 45 | The KonMari Method
3 ways to declutter your business life

Success is often associated with accumulation – more clients, projects, and profits in business. However, the KonMari Method,[80] popularized by Marie Kondo[81] in her quest for decluttering homes, can be an unexpected but transformative tool for entrepreneurs and professionals.

By adapting the KonMari principles to the business world, we can create a workplace that sparks joy, drives productivity, and cultivates fulfillment and contentment.

Create room for growth.

The KonMari Method teaches us that to appreciate and find joy in our possessions truly, we must first let go of the clutter. This philosophy can easily be applied to business. It's all about decluttering[82] your business practices, focusing on what truly matters, and shedding what no longer serves your goals. Move from a To-Do List to an Action Items List orientation.

Consider your project portfolio. What projects no longer align with your company's mission or goals? What products or services aren't performing as expected?

Just as you declutter your home by saying goodbye to items that no longer spark joy, eliminate these aspects from your business.

Act.

One common trap in the business world is endless planning. While planning is crucial for success, it can quickly become a form of procrastination, preventing us from acting.

The KonMari Method emphasizes the importance of action over contemplation. When you focus on doing rather than overthinking, you'll discover the true potential of your business. You'll learn from your actions, adapt to challenges, and achieve results.

This shift from planning to doing can be a game-changer for your business's growth. My predecessor was known widely as the "Get Shit Done" guy. He was regularly activated to perform, accomplish, but most of all, to act.

A bias for action – and the term "chunking" – was introduced as an attribute of excellence in the 1980s in In Search of Excellence: Lessons from America's Best-Run Companies[83] by Thomas Peters & Robert Waterman.

In the book, the authors relay a story of an Exxon line officer's "remarkable tale of improvement." The officer had reported on a series of pragmatic actions, knocking off one problem at a time. "Was it a tale of shrewd foresight and bold strategic moves? Not in our view," the authors state. "It was a classic example of what we have come to call the 'theory of chunks.' We have come to believe that the key success factor in business is simply getting one's arms around almost any practical problem and knocking it off – now." Chunk your Outlook calendar too. Segment into time bands to optimize your energy, focus, and attention—block time to counter the potential of being a hamster on a treadmill to your schedule.

Seek joy.

Above all, the KonMari Method encourages us to seek joy[84] in our surroundings. This translates to finding joy in your work and your created environment in business.

Joyful companies are often more productive, creative, and successful. Employees who enjoy their work are more motivated, engaged, and willing to go the extra mile. This is especially important today when nearly eight out of ten people go to work every day disengaged or passionately disengaged.

Customers can also sense this joy, increasing loyalty and creating a positive brand perception. They become raving fans – emotionally connected to the brand.

Overall, the KonMari Method isn't just about tidying up physical spaces; it can also be a powerful tool for enhancing your business.

> Ask yourself and your team, "Are we delighted with what we're doing?"

By giving up what no longer serves you, shifting from planning to action (doing), and seeking joy, you can create a business that sparks joy for you and your team and drives long-term success.

So, declutter your business and your life, embrace a bias for action and speed, and let the joy of entrepreneurship guide your path to prosperity.

End Notes for Personal & Business Development Section

1. Molly Oswaks, "Over 3 million People Took This Course on Happiness. Here's What Some Learned.," *The New York Times*, March 13, 2021, sec. Style, https://www.nytimes.com/2021/03/13/style/happiness-course.html.
2. David Flach, "The Cost of Lost Productivity," Bloomfire, December 8, 2021, https://bloomfire.com/blog/lost-productivity/.
3. Matthew Kelly, *The Rhythm of Life: Living Every Day with Passion & Purpose*, 3rd ed. edition (Blue Sparrow, 2015).
4. Bryan Robinson Ph.D, "New Research Shows Remote And Hybrid Workers Suffering Physical And Mental Health Dilemmas," Forbes, accessed September 22, 2023, https://www.forbes.com/sites/bryanrobinson/2021/11/01/new-research-shows-remote-and-hybrid-workers-suffering-physical-and-mental-health-dilemmas/.
5. "Next Big Idea Club: The Hand-Picking Ideas Authors Book Club," Next Big Idea Club, accessed September 22, 2023, https://nextbigideaclub.com/.
6. Gallup Inc, "How to Measure Employee Engagement With the Q12," Gallup.com, accessed September 22, 2023, https://www.gallup.com/workplace/356045/q12-question-summary.aspx.
7. "Walker Tracker Employee Wellness," *Terryberry* (blog), accessed September 22, 2023, https://www.terryberry.com/walker-tracker/.
8. "(5) Instant Gratification Generation in the Workforce | LinkedIn," accessed September 25, 2023, https://www.linkedin.com/pulse/instant-gratification-generation-workforce-victoria-parker/.
9. Kori D. Miller, "5+ Ways to Develop a Growth Mindset Using Grit & Resilience," PositivePsychology.com, January 30, 2020, https://positivepsychology.com/5-ways-develop-grit-resilience/.
10. Angela Duckworth, *Grit: The Power of Passion and Perseverance*, Grit: The Power of Passion and Perseverance (New York, NY, US: Scribner/Simon & Schuster, 2016).
11. "Success Story Of Bill Gates – A Life Filled With Successes," November 6, 2020, https://businessconnectindia.in/bill-gates-success-story/.
12. Danny Meyer, *Setting the Table: The Transforming Power of Hospitality in Business*, Reprint edition (New York: Ecco, 2008).
13. "Leading Equity Crowdfunding Platforms for 2023 - CrowdFunding.Guide," March 1, 2022, https://www.crowdfunding.guide/

leading-equity-crowdfunding-platforms/, https://www.crowdfunding.guide/leading-equity-crowdfunding-platforms/.

14. "What Are the Pros and Cons of Crowdfunding Platforms for Inventors?," accessed September 29, 2023, https://www.linkedin.com/advice/1/what-pros-cons-crowdfunding-platforms-inventors-skills-inventio n.
15. "Creating a Crowdfunding Campaign Plan (With Steps and Tips) | Indeed.Com," accessed September 29, 2023, https://www.indeed.com/career-advice/career-development/crowdfunding-campaign-plan.
16. *UF Innovate Fast Break Ventures Summit 2022*, 2022, https://www.youtube.com/watch?v=b3qtgGnygcQ.
17. AllBusiness, "A Guide To Investor Pitch Decks For Startup Fundraising," Forbes, accessed September 29, 2023, https://www.forbes.com/sites/allbusiness/2020/06/20/guide-to-investor-pitch-decks-for-startup-fundr aising/.
18. "The 4H's of Pitching: How 2 Pitch to Investors," Living Entrepreneurship Blog, October 2, 2019, https://blogs.babson.edu/entrepreneurship/2019/10/02/the-4hs-of-pitching-how-2-pitch-to-investors/
19. "About Us | Scrub Daddy | America's Favorite Sponge Company," accessed March 29, 2024, https://scrubdaddy.com/about/.
20. "What Is an Unfair Advantage? | Ask LEANSTACK," accessed September 29, 2023, https://ask.leanstack.com/en/articles/904720-what-is-an-unfair-advantage.
21. Britt Skrabanek, "How to Write a Meaningful Value Proposition (With Examples)," ClearVoice, May 26, 2020, https://www.clearvoice.com/resources/what-is-a-value-proposition/.
22. "Target Market: Examples and How To Define It | Indeed.Com," accessed September 29, 2023, https://www.indeed.com/career-advice/career-development/target-market-examples.
23. Debi Kleiman, *First Pitch: Winning Money, Mentors, and More for Your Startup* (Babson College Publishing, 2020).
24. Seth Godin, *Purple Cow: Transform Your Business by Being Remarkable*, First Edition (London: Penguin, 2005).
25. "Sarasota, Florida - Van Wezel Performing Arts Hall," accessed September 29, 2023, https://www.vanwezel.org/.
26. Susan David, "Susan David: The Gift and Power of Emotional Courage | TED Talk," accessed September 29, 2023, https://www.ted.com/talks/susan_david_the_gift_and_power_of_emotional_courage.
27. "Netflix Culture — Seeking Excellence," accessed September 29, 2023, https://jobs.netflix.com/culture.

28. "Shark Tank Products - Every Product from the Show," Shark Tank Products, September 22, 2023, https://allsharktankproducts.com/.
29. "What Is a Business Model with Types and Examples," Investopedia, accessed September 29, 2023, https://www.investopedia.com/terms/b/businessmodel.asp.
30. "Customer Acquisition Cost vs. Lifetime Value (With Examples) | Indeed.Com," accessed September 29, 2023, https://www.indeed.com/career-advice/career-development/customer-acquisition-cost-vs-lifetime-value.
31. "Acquisition.Com Home," accessed November 6, 2023, https://www.acquisition.com.
32. Christina Piccoli, "How to Brainwash Yourself to Success," *Medium* (blog), February 9, 2023, https://medium.com/@christinapiccoli/how-to-brainwash-yourself-to-success-a9fea18a21c0.
33. "(1) 4-Ways to Build Self-Efficacy in Your Business | LinkedIn," accessed November 6, 2023, https://www.linkedin.com/pulse/4-ways-build-self-efficacy-your-business-rory-tempest/.
34. Nina Zipkin, "22 Successful Entrepreneurs Share What Inspires Them to Keep Going," Entrepreneur, June 13, 2019, https://www.entrepreneur.com/living/22-successful-entrepreneurs-share-what-inspires-them-to/290029.
35. "Delta Family Takes Fresh Inspiration from 40th Birthday of Famed Spirit of Delta 767 Aircraft | Delta News Hub," accessed November 6, 2023, https://news.delta.com/delta-family-takes-fresh-inspiration-40th-birthday-famed-spirit-delta-767-aircraft.
36. "18 Self-Care Tips for Busy People – Georgia HOPE," accessed September 29, 2023, https://gahope.org/18-self-care-tips-for-busy-people/.
37. "How To Create Work-Life Balance," Cleveland Clinic, April 27, 2022, https://health.clevelandclinic.org/work-life-balance/.
38. Max Lyadvinsky, "Startups Need More Than Money to Succeed -- They Need Smart Money," Entrepreneur, November 16, 2018, https://www.entrepreneur.com/money-finance/startups-need-more-than-money-to-succeed-they-need-smart/323018.
39. YEC, "Council Post: A Review Of The Minimum Viable Product Approach," Forbes, accessed November 6, 2023, https://www.forbes.com/sites/theyec/2021/12/08/a-review-of-the-minimum-viable-product-approach/.
40. "My Experiments in Lean Pricing – by Ash Maurya – StudentsTry," accessed November 6, 2023, https://littlesteves.wordpress.com/2015/04/25/my-experiments-in-lean-pricing-by-ash-maurya/.

41 "Pricing Strategies," accessed November 6, 2023, https://www.indeed.com/.
42 "#NACCE2023 - National Association for Community College Entrepreneurship," accessed November 6, 2023, https://www.nacce.com/events/nacce2023.
43 Binit Acharya, "The Guerrilla Marketing Campaign That Caused City-Wide Panic in Boston," Medium, September 16, 2020, https://bettermarketing.pub/the-guerrilla-marketing-campaign-that-caused-city-wide-panic-in-boston-9daeeff39101.
44 "RadioShack To Rebrand As 'The Shack'? - Slashdot," accessed November 17, 2023, https://slashdot.org/story/09/08/03/135227/radioshack-to-rebrand-as-the-shack.
45 "#RaceTogether: Starbucks' Attempt to Discuss Race in America and Its Impact on Company Reputation and Employees | Institute for Public Relations," accessed November 17, 2023, https://instituteforpr.org/racetogether-starbucks-attempt-to-discuss-race-in-america-and-its-impact- on-company-reputation-and-employees/.
46 Lindsay Blakely, "My Company Grew Too Fast -- and Went Out of Business - CBS News," August 12, 2010, http://www.cbsnews.com/8301-505143_162-40241795/my-company-grew-too-fast----and-went-out-of-business/.
47 "5 Companies That Grew Too Quickly (and What You Can Learn From Them)," Entrepreneur, March 12, 2018, https://www.entrepreneur.com/growing-a-business/5-companies-that-grew-too-quickly-and-what-you-can-learn/310166.
48 Rita McGrath and Alexander van Putten, "How to Set More-Realistic Growth Targets," *Harvard Business Review*, July 12, 2017, https://hbr.org/2017/07/how-to-set-more-realistic-growth-targets.
49 "Jim Collins - Concepts - Confront The Brutal Facts," accessed February 2, 2024, https://www.jimcollins.com/concepts/confront-the-brutal-facts.html.
50 Expert Panel®, "Council Post: 14 Factors To Research Before Entering A New Business Market," Forbes, accessed February 2, 2024, https://www.forbes.com/sites/forbesbusinessdevelopmentcouncil/2022/01/24/14-factors-to-research-before-entering-a-new-business-market/.
51 "What Is Omni-Channel? 20 Top Omni-Channel Experience Examples," September 6, 2023, https://blog.hubspot.com/service/omni-channel-experience.
52 "11 Effective Strategies To Find Opportunities in Business | Indeed.Com," accessed February 16, 2024, https://www.indeed.com/career-advice/career-development/finding-opportunities.

53 Steve Olenski, "6 Tips For Hiring The Right Employee," Forbes, accessed February 16, 2024, https://www.forbes.com/sites/steveolenski/2015/05/15/6-tips-for-hiring-the-right-employee/.
54 "(7) Bill Gates 1st Startup Traf-O-Data Was a Failure in 70's – Failure Is Just a Word If You Look Back at Your Mistakes | LinkedIn," accessed February 23, 2024, https://www.linkedin.com/pulse/bill-gates-1st-startup-traf-o-data-failure-70s-just-danial/.
55 Stephen Gerard, "Author Post: Fail Fast And Fail Forward ... Learn By Doing!," Forbes, accessed February 23, 2024, https://www.forbes.com/sites/forbesbooksauthors/2021/07/29/fail-fast-and-fail-forward--learn-by-doi ng/.
56 Young Entrepreneur Council, "How to Remove Emotions From the Business Equation," Forbes, accessed February 23, 2024, https://www.forbes.com/sites/yec/2011/06/27/how-to-remove-emotions-from-the-business-equation/.
57 Matthew Toren, "3 Ways Owning Your Mistakes Will Make You Powerful," Entrepreneur, March 24, 2014, https://www.entrepreneur.com/growing-a-business/3-ways-owning-your-mistakes-will-make-you-po werful/232417.
58 Entrepreneur Staff, "How 15 People in Their 20s Built Million-Dollar Businesses," Entrepreneur, August 24, 2021, https://www.entrepreneur.com/growing-a-business/how-15-people-in-their-20s-built-million-dollar-businesses/380002.
59 Chris Carosa, "Why Successful Entrepreneurs Need To Be Calculated Risk Takers," Forbes, accessed March 1, 2024, https://www.forbes.com/sites/chriscarosa/2020/08/07/why-successful-entrepreneurs-need-to-be-calculated-risk-takers/.
60 "The Ultimate Guide to Setting Business Goals - 2024," MasterClass, accessed March 4,2024, https://www.masterclass.com/articles/the-ultimate-guide-to-setting-business-goals.
61 Expert Panel, "Council Post: How To Set Realistic Business Goals That Will Still Help Employees Grow," Forbes, accessed March 4, 2024, https://www.forbes.com/sites/theyec/2021/10/22/how-to-set-realistic-business-goals-that-will-still-he lp-employees-grow/.
62 "7 Reasons to Dream Big and Start Small | LinkedIn," accessed March 4, 2024, https://www.linkedin.com/pulse/7-reasons-dream-big-start-small-steve-siegfried/.
63 "7 Unorthodox Rituals of Successful Entrepreneurs | Talk Business," accessed March 18, 2024, https://www.talk-business.co.uk/2014/11/30/7-unorthodox-rituals-successful-entrepreneurs/.

64 "10 Reasons Why Collaboration Is Important in the Workplace | Indeed.Com," accessed March 18, 2024, https://www.indeed.com/career-advice/career-development/why-is-collaboration-important.

65 Jordan Hart, "Mark Cuban Says He Avoids Wasting Time at Work, and That Meetings Are the Main Culprit," Business Insider, accessed March 18, 2024, https://www.businessinsider.com/mark-cuban-avoids-meetings-and-phone-calls-at-work-2023-7.

66 Alison Coleman, "The Art Of Bootstrapping: Four Entrepreneurs Share Their Secrets," Forbes, accessed March 26, 2024, https://www.forbes.com/sites/alisoncoleman/2022/03/17/the-art-of-bootstrapping-four-entrepreneurs-share-their-secrets/.

67 "3 Ways to Overcome Impostor Syndrome in the Workplace," accessed March 26, 2024, https://www.indeed.com/lead/impostor-syndrome.

68 Tony Schwartz, "How to Think Creatively," *Harvard Business Review*, November 14, 2011, https://hbr.org/2011/11/how-to-think-creatively.

69 "Early-Stage Entrepreneurship," Kauffman Indicators of Entrepreneurship, accessed April 1, 2024, https://indicators.kauffman.org/.

70 "The No. 1 Reason Most Entrepreneurs Start Businesses - Businessnewsdaily.Com."

71 Scott Miker, "4 Reasons Following Your Passion Leads to Success," Entrepreneur, March 19, 2022, https://www.entrepreneur.com/leadership/4-reasons-following-your-passion-leads-to-success/419610.

72 "(54) 4 Ways a Business Can Create a Positive Social Impact | LinkedIn," accessed April 1, 2024, https://www.linkedin.com/pulse/4-ways-business-can-create-positive-social-impact-aitzaz-ahmed/.

73 "(27) Perseverance in Business: A Strength or a Threat to Achieving Effectiveness? | LinkedIn," accessed April 15, 2024, https://www.linkedin.com/pulse/perseverance-business-strength-threat-achieving-business-coach/.

74 Robin Bruce, "Discovering Your Purpose In Business And Life," Forbes, accessed April 15, 2024, https://www.forbes.com/sites/robinbruce/2015/08/23/discovering-your-purpose/.

75 "9 Ways to Cultivate Inner Strength and Resilience | Tony Robbins," accessed April 15, 2024, https://www.tonyrobbins.com/business/inner-strength/.

76 "Wheel of Life Interactive Assessment Landing Page," accessed April 15, 2024, https://core.tonyrobbins.com/wheel-of-life.

77 Eric J. McNulty, "The Other 'F' Word: An Interview with John Danner," Strategy+business, accessed April

15, 2024, https://www.strategy-business.com/blog/The-Other-F-Word-An-Interview-with-John-Danner.

78 Amanda Morin, "What Is Growth Mindset?," Understood, accessed April 15, 2024, https://www.understood.org/en/articles/growth-mindset.

79 Farnam Street, "Carol Dweck: A Summary of Growth and Fixed Mindsets," Farnam Street, March 2, 2015, https://fs.blog/carol-dweck-mindset/.

80 "About the KonMari Method – KonMari | The Official Website of Marie Kondo," accessed April 22, 2024, https://konmari.com/about-the-konmari-method/.

81 Taffy Brodesser-Akner, "Marie Kondo, Tidying Up and the Ruthless War on Stuff," *The New York Times*, July 6, 2016, sec. Magazine, https://www.nytimes.com/2016/07/10/magazine/marie-kondo-and-the-ruthless-war-on-stuff.html.

82 "How to Use Marie Kondo's Decluttering Principles in Your Business | SCORE," accessed April 22, 2024, https://www.score.org/resource/blog-post/how-use-marie-kondo%E2%80%99s-decluttering-principles-your-business.

83 "In Search of Excellence by Tom Peters and Robert Waterman | Thrive Street Leadership Library," Thrive Street Advisors, accessed April 22, 2024, https://www.thrivestreetadvisors.com/leadership-library/in-search-of-excellence.

84 "(26) Finding Joy After Decluttering | LinkedIn," accessed April 22, 2024, https://www.linkedin.com/pulse/finding-joy-after-decluttering-marie-kondo/.

5. Networking & Relationship Building
In Brief

Networking and relationship building are essential in both the personal and professional spheres, facilitating opportunities for collaboration, growth, and mutual support. In today's interconnected world, cultivating a robust network and fostering meaningful connections are essential for success. Effective networking involves more than simply collecting contacts - genuine engagement, active listening, and promoting trust. Relationships built on authenticity and reciprocity open doors to new opportunities and contribute to a sense of personal fulfillment. This section explores the art of networking and relationship building, uncovering their profound impact and strategic nuances in various contexts.

Super Hack 46 | Get Stronger Together
Networking can propel your career to new heights

In a world where connectivity seems to shrink the distance between individuals, networking is indispensable for professional growth and success. From learning from industry peers and finding mentors to sharing skills and knowledge, networking offers invaluable personal and professional development opportunities. By embracing networking as a proactive strategy, individuals can tap into a wealth of insights, experiences, and connections that propel them toward new heights.

> **Self-Assessment Questions:**
>
> 1. Have you actively engaged in networking to learn from others in your industry, participate in industry-related conversations, and expose yourself to diverse ideas and emerging trends to broaden your knowledge base and stay updated with advancements in your field?
>
> 2. Have you sought out and established connections with potential mentors within your professional network, expressing your eagerness to learn and benefit from their insights and guidance in your career?
>
> 3. Are you actively sharing your skills, knowledge, and resources within your professional network, fostering mutually beneficial relationships, and contributing to the growth of others in your industry while enhancing your reputation as a collaborative and valuable community member?

Super Hack 46 | Get Stronger Together
Networking can propel your career to new heights

In the old days, there were six degrees of separation between two people. With social media and all the available connected platforms, I have said it is half of the degree of separation between any two people.

It often feels like a small world, for sure. I see it in conversations and interactions with strangers or people I know well. The connection might be related to where I grew up, went to school, a former employer, or someone in a previous job who worked for a former boss of mine.

These coincidences pop up everywhere, and I am sure in your life, too.

When I started in the incubation industry, I relied on networking at industry conferences, speaking at workshops, and attending professional development functions.

Today, my network takes me to all parts of the globe, forming connections and relationships effortlessly and in real time and producing tangible value. Because I cast a wide net to find and leverage value in my network, I have discovered resources for our clients, learned about innovative programs to improve our programs, and made referrals.

I can better build authentic relationships by having insights into our visitors and VIPs and what matters to them. How do I get these insights? I receive briefs about these potential connections and possibilities every day **before** I meet with people I don't know.

Networking has become indispensable for professional growth and success in today's interconnected world. Networking enables individuals to learn from others in their industry, find mentors, and establish valuable connections.

Let's explore the significance of these three networking aspects and how they can propel your career to new heights.

Learn from others in your industry.

One of the most significant advantages of networking is the opportunity to learn from others in your industry. When you engage with professionals who possess different perspectives, experiences, and expertise, you gain valuable insights that can broaden your knowledge base.

Networking events, conferences, and online communities offer platforms to connect with like-minded individuals and engage in meaningful discussions.

LinkedIn[1] has multiple industry-specific groups for people to join. Whatever your professional interests, you will likely find a fit for you. If your interest is highly niche, then maybe not; however, others like you probably want to discuss the same topic and have yet to find a group. Don't be afraid to create your tribe (group) and start the conversation.

You expose yourself to diverse ideas and emerging trends by actively participating in industry-related conversations. These interactions keep you updated with your field's latest advancements and best practices.

Moreover, networking opens doors to collaborative learning opportunities, where you can collaborate on projects, share resources, and benefit from collective expertise. Embracing a learning mindset within your networking efforts fosters personal and professional growth, enabling you to evolve in your chosen field continuously.

I met some of my closest friends through industry trade associations, and some of the best professional experiences I have had were through participation in membership organizations or a position on an advisory board.

Find a mentor.

A mentor can be a game-changer in your career journey. Networking provides a platform for finding and connecting with mentors who can guide and support your professional development. Mentors are individuals who have walked the path you aspire to traverse, and their insights and advice can prove invaluable.

Networking events and industry-specific gatherings are excellent environments for identifying potential mentors. Engage in conversations, ask questions, and express your eagerness to learn.

Establishing genuine connections with experienced professionals increases the likelihood of finding a mentor who resonates with your goals and can offer guidance tailored to your needs.

Some of the most successful entrepreneurs you know have had mentors.[2] Mark Zuckerberg, co-founder and CEO of Facebook, has discussed how Steve Jobs helped shape him into who he is today. Jobs assisted him through unsure times and showed him that he could try to change the world (but not necessarily for the common good).

My mentor (and friend) was substantially older than me, but he taught me valuable lessons about people, coached me through challenging workplace issues, and inspired me to be a better version of myself. He lived his life in stage 3 (legacy). He had long completed the stages of success and significance. If you are evaluating your own life, a terrific book to learn more about these stages is Bob Buford's Half-Time.[3] to put the third stage into practice – legacy – ask yourself this critical question, "**How do I want to be remembered?**"

Sharing is caring.

Networking facilitates the creation of meaningful connections. You establish relationships built on mutual trust and respect by engaging with professionals in and out of your field. These connections can lead to collaborations, partnerships, and even job opportunities.

> Like you would in Vegas, place your bets. Find what gives you joy and inspiration – whether professional development, industry association participation, learning journeys, reading, attending trade shows, or taking online classes.

Furthermore, networking provides a platform for sharing skills and knowledge. Connecting with others lets you exchange expertise, ideas, and resources. By sharing your skills, you contribute to the growth of others in your industry while enhancing your reputation.

This symbiotic relationship strengthens the professional community, fostering an environment where individuals can thrive and get better together.

Networking is a powerful catalyst for professional growth, enabling individuals to learn from others in their industry, find mentors, and build valuable networks and connections.

Embracing networking as a proactive tool empowers you to tap into the vast knowledge and experiences that can elevate your career and venture to new heights.

When I hear new heights, I think of the following Dr. Seuss lines from his book, **Oh, The Places You'll Go**[4] (and this book is appropriate for more than graduation gifts):

You have brains in your head.
You have feet in your shoes.
You can steer yourself.
Any direction you choose.
You're on your own. And you know what you know.
And **YOU** are the person who'll decide where to go.

Opportunities await. You need to determine where you want to go.

Super Hack 47 | All for One and One for All
What can you do to benefit others?

Networking has become a cornerstone of success, but what does it mean to network effectively? It's about forging genuine connections and fostering relationships that benefit all parties. Collaboration lies at the heart of successful networking. Rather than transactional interactions, genuine relationship-building involves offering value and creating meaningful content that resonates with your audience.

Self-Assessment Questions:

1. When engaging with potential business partners or clients, do you actively consider what unique skills, knowledge, or resources you can offer to set yourself apart from others and establish a solid foundation for mutually beneficial relationships?

2. Are you consistently creating and sharing valuable content that educates, inspires, and entertains your target audience, positioning yourself as a reliable source of information or a thought leader rather than focusing solely on self-promotion?

3. Do you strongly emphasize retaining and engaging existing customers, keeping them updated on your latest developments, seeking their feedback, and delivering excellent and memorable customer experiences to build a loyal customer base and foster positive word-of-mouth in your network?

Super Hack 47 | All for One and One for All
What can you do to benefit others?

In today's fast-paced business world, networking has become an indispensable tool for individuals and organizations. We've discussed it a bit in my previous hacks, but how do you truly network successfully?

It is about making connections and cultivating meaningful relationships that can lead to mutual growth and success for all parties involved. And *collaboration*?

I have always thought *collaboration* was an overused buzzword. The best collaborations are where we invest in each other's *mutual outcomes and get better together.* This is both hard and rare. It is hard because it requires you to "subvene" your self-interests. It is rare because most non-profit organizations possess a scarcity mindset. Symmetry and reciprocity make collaboration successful —such successful partnerships are rare because they involve giving up some of your identity and prioritizing for the benefit of others.

Today, collaboration is touted in the nonprofit world. Still, when you lift the car's hood, you often see an asymmetrical relationship or one organization "winning" (although nonprofits are told not to think this way) at the expense of the other.

I suggest something better.

What do you have to offer?

Consider <u>networking as a two-way street</u>.[5] While making connections is essential, offering something valuable in return is equally important. When engaging with potential business partners or clients, ask yourself what unique skills, knowledge, or resources you bring.

What can you offer that sets you apart from others?

Recognizing your strengths and expertise can position you as an asset in networking. Whether providing industry insights, offering professional advice, or sharing relevant connections, having something to offer establishes a solid foundation for mutually beneficial relationships.

Remember, networking is not just about taking; it's about building a community where everyone benefits.

Transactional interactions should be understood when building relationships. The amount of spam generated through LinkedIn is incredible. Someone sends you an offensive InMail to bait you to respond. See a recent one I received:

"I went through my emails and noticed you still need to respond. This indicates the following:

- A giant T-Rex is chasing you and hasn't had time to respond.

- You are interested but haven't had time to respond.

- You have no interest. Whichever one it is, please let me know, as I'm getting worried!"

So, why should I respond to a message like this one? It offered no value to me. It displayed no understanding of my business or my needs. It showed no appreciation for the hundreds of emails I receive each day. Nothing in this email made it rise above spam.

Create helpful content.

Content creation has become a powerful networking tool in today's digital era. Instead of solely focusing on self-promotion, shift your mindset toward providing beneficial content to your target audience. Share your expertise through blog posts, articles, podcasts, or videos that address their pain points and offer practical solutions.

YouTube, Facebook, Instagram, TikTok, LinkedIn, Medium.... Those platforms and more are full of content creators sharing valuable information and engaging people worldwide.

Reflect on your professional experience and determine how to leverage its best to create media your audience will find helpful. Figure out how to be a resource and depot for others.

By positioning yourself as a reliable source of information or thought leader, you establish credibility and trust in your network. Your content should aim to educate, inspire, and entertain rather than be solely promotional.

Keep customers engaged and loyal.

Networking is not limited to making new connections but also nurtures existing personal and business relationships. <u>You need to retain customers and gain new ones</u> [6]

> By consistently delivering value through your media content, you attract like-minded individuals and potential business partners who resonate with your message and will likely engage and collaborate with you.

Remember to stay in touch with past customers and clients, as they can become valuable advocates for your business. Keep them updated on your latest developments, offer exclusive upselling opportunities, discounts, or promotions, and seek their feedback to demonstrate that their satisfaction and engagement matter.

Similarly, consider the power of customer retention.

Happy and satisfied customers are more likely to refer your business to others, creating a positive ripple effect in your network. Invest in providing excellent and memorable customer experiences, promptly address concerns or service shortfalls, and continually seek ways to enhance their experiences (and how to connect them to your brand).

By focusing on customer engagement, you build a loyal customer base and open doors to new opportunities through positive word-of-mouth.

Networking in business is more than just exchanging business cards or making connections on social media. It requires a proactive approach and genuine efforts to build lasting relationships.

Realize the need to offer value, create helpful media content, and nurture existing customers, and by doing so, harness the power of networking to drive growth and success in your business.

Embrace the art of networking and watch your professional network flourish.

Super Hack 48 | You Only Get One First Impression
Make it positive by mastering these 3 things

First impressions are made in seconds; mastering the art of making a positive impact is crucial. Whether it's a job interview, a networking event, or a chance encounter, those initial moments can shape how others perceive you and influence the opportunities that come your way. In today's digital age, where pre-impressions are just as important as in-person interactions, curating your brand carefully is essential.

> **Self-Assessment Questions:**
>
> 1. Do you consciously work on projecting confidence through your body language, such as maintaining eye contact, offering a firm handshake, and speaking clearly and confidently to inspire trust and respect in your interactions with others?
>
> 2. Are you consistently approachable, warm, and friendly, trying to show your smile and maintain an open posture when engaging with people while actively listening, asking thoughtful questions, and engaging in meaningful conversations to create a positive and welcoming atmosphere?
>
> 3. When attending different events or occasions, do you pay attention to dressing appropriately for the specific setting, demonstrating respect for the event and the people involved, and striking a balance between your style and appropriateness to make a lasting and positive first impression?

Super Hack 48 | You Only Get One First Impression
Make it positive by mastering these 3 things

It takes a mere seven seconds to make a first impression.

Imagine a job interview on Zoom. The dog is barking in the background, your internet is spotty, and you spilled your drink all over your laptop. You are frantically cleaning up and trying to mentally get in the zone for an interactive conversation with your potential future boss.

While you might receive empathy, you never get a second chance to make a first impression, and it's those initial moments that can shape how others perceive you.

An excellent first impression is crucial whether attending a job interview, meeting new people, or even going on a first date. It sets the tone for future interactions and can significantly impact the opportunities that come your way.

If you make a terrible first impression, you might still change others' opinions of you by making a good impression next time—but remember, it's essential to be consistent.

A pre-impression has become the new first impression in our digital world. Many of us initially interact with people in our network through Facebook, Instagram, or LinkedIn. But you can be sure some people conduct a simple Google search on you before meeting in person. What are they finding? How do you want strangers to perceive your "personal brand"?

Please don't make the mistake of merely deleting something on social media, thinking you're erasing it from your digital history. **Your digital footprint follows you for your entire lifetime.**

Sometimes, what you erase makes a bigger impression than what remains.

Put your best foot forward at every stage of building a good impression. I'd suggest three ways you can improve that impression.

Confidence is key.

Confidence[7] is magnetic, drawing people toward you and giving them faith in your abilities. When you exude self-assurance, you inspire trust and often receive respect. It is no wonder that confidence is one of Gallup's Ten business builder talents.

By projecting confidence, you show others that you believe in yourself, instilling confidence in them.

Show your smile.

Being approachable, warm, and friendly goes a long way in creating a positive first impression. Smile! You may not be on Candid Camera, but you are being recorded by the eyes of people who meet you.

Extroverted individuals are often perceived as pleasant, engaging, and ready to connect. Smiling and maintaining an open posture, signaling your willingness to interact. Then, show genuine interest in others by actively listening, asking thoughtful and insightful questions, and engaging in meaningful conversations.

> One way to exhibit confidence is through body language. Stand tall, make eye contact, and offer a firm handshake when appropriate. Additionally, speak clearly and confidently, expressing your thoughts and ideas without hesitation.

And keep smiling. Remember, a friendly demeanor can help alleviate tension and foster a comfortable environment for everyone involved. Smiling invites others in and provides a warm and welcoming energy.

Dress your best…for the occasion.

While we should never judge a book by its cover, our attire sends powerful signals about who we are and how seriously we take certain situations.

Dressing appropriately[8] for an event demonstrates respect for the occasion and the people involved. Whether it's a professional setting, a social gathering, or a casual outing, aim to balance personal style and appropriateness, not too underdressed or overdressed.

While casual business attire is often the go-to business standard, know your audience and their values when deciding your appearance etiquette. A boundaryless culture still requires you to look and feel your best.

In the realm of first impressions, it's to understand the impact we can make on others in those initial moments. Exhibiting confidence, being extroverted and friendly, and dressing appropriately are crucial elements in creating a positive and lasting impression.

Embodying these qualities can cultivate trust, forge meaningful connections, and open doors to countless opportunities.

Every interaction is an opportunity to showcase the best version of yourself. While first impressions are important, being authentic and genuine in your interactions is equally essential.

Combining these qualities with sincerity, empathy, and respect will make a great first impression and lay the foundation for meaningful and lasting relationships in your personal and professional spheres.

Super Hack 49 | Back to Basics
Follow these tips to simplify your journey to success

Take a refreshing approach to entrepreneurial wisdom by revisiting the timeless lessons learned from the simplicity of running a lemonade stand. From the humble beginnings of childhood entrepreneurship to the towering success stories of corporate giants like Apple, we uncover the fundamental principles that underpin achievement. Starting small, embracing resilience, and understanding your audience are just a few invaluable lessons from this classic summertime endeavor.

> **Self-Assessment Questions:**
>
> 1. Are you embracing the concept of "thinking big, starting small, and scaling fast" in your entrepreneurial journey, breaking down big dreams into manageable tasks, and celebrating each small milestone?
>
> 2. How do you handle setbacks or rejection in your business endeavors? Are you resilient, viewing setbacks as opportunities to learn, adapt, pivot, and improve rather than failures?
>
> 3. Have you identified your target market and tailored your sales approach to meet the needs and preferences of your customers? Are you focusing on the right audience to maximize the value delivered to those genuinely interested in your product or service?

Super Hack 49 | Back to Basics
Follow these tips to simplify your journey to success

When looking for the most valuable entrepreneurial lessons, sometimes we must look outside the boardrooms and business schools and return to basics.

Envisioning a lemonade stand is a great way to get into this mindset.

You might have even had your own in your early days of entrepreneurship. By harkening back to this simple summer activity, you can uncover lost fundamental principles that can guide you on the journey to success.

It is okay to start small.

Kids operating a lemonade stand start small, focusing only on selling one ice-cold refreshment at a time. They don't aim to conquer the world immediately but focus on a simple yet achievable goal: selling refreshing lemonade to neighbors. My coaching advice to business builders is always to think big, start small, and scale fast. As one of my colleagues always reminds me, start. The activation is what is so important.

> Focusing on these smaller milestones allows you to step back down the road and see how these small steps culminate in success.

By starting small, they gain valuable experience, can test their ideas, and learn from their mistakes. As aspiring entrepreneurs, we can embrace this lesson by breaking down our big dreams into manageable tasks and celebrating each small milestone.

A great example of this is Apple,[9] "the world's first corporation to close with a market value above $3 trillion."

While this is an incredible milestone, it started differently. After beginning in a California garage, the company struggled for years before Steve Jobs rescued it through action and consistency, bringing it from near bankruptcy to the blockbuster company it is today.

Fun Fact: Microsoft infused $150 million into Apple when it was close to failing.

Don't overthink.

The resilience children possess when running a lemonade stand is genuinely inspiring. Despite facing rejection or setbacks, they bounce back with unwavering optimism. Kids understand that "no" doesn't mean failure; it simply means an opportunity to learn, adapt, pivot, and improve.

Entrepreneurs can benefit significantly from adopting this mindset. Instead of dwelling on setbacks or becoming disheartened by rejections, viewing them as learning experiences is crucial. Each "no" brings you closer to a "yes."

As a kid, I often said, "No is just not yes yet." This philosophy certainly fatigued my parents.

Often in sales, you'll receive a lot more "no's" than "yes's." Being resilient and learning to handle[10] rejections properly can allow you to increase success in the long run. You become attuned to finding ways to improve your sales strategies, as opposed to feeling defeated.

It's all about the way you perceive the situation.

Who's buying? The best investor is a paying customer.

Kids running a lemonade stand quickly learn an important lesson about their customers: only some passing by are potential buyers.

Children observe the people who show interest, stop to chat, or eagerly reach for their wallets. They learn to recognize their target audience and tailor their sales approach accordingly.

Similarly, entrepreneurs must identify their target market and understand their <u>customers' needs and preferences</u>.[11] Entrepreneurs can save time, resources, and effort by focusing on the right audience while delivering value to those who genuinely want their product or service.

Running a simple lemonade stand might seem like child's play, but the entrepreneurial lessons it imparts are anything but trivial.

The next time you see kids running a lemonade stand, take a moment to observe and learn from their intuitive entrepreneurial spirit. After all, even the smallest ventures can teach us the greatest lessons.

End Notes for Networking & Relationship Building Section

1. "LinkedIn Groups Membership," LinkedIn Help, accessed September 29, 2023, https://www.linkedin.com/help/linkedin/answer/a540824/linkedin-groups-membership-overview?lang=en-us&intendedLocale=en.
2. "Three Famous Billionaire Entrepreneurs and Their Mentors," *Small Business BC* (blog), accessed September 29, 2023, https://smallbusinessbc.ca/article/three-famous-billionaire-entrepreneurs-and-their-mentors/.
3. "Halftime: Moving from Success to Significance: Buford, Bob P., Jim Collins: 9780310344445: Amazon.Com: Books," accessed September 29, 2023, https://www.amazon.com/Halftime-Significance-Bob-P-Buford/dp/0310344441.
4. "Amazon.com: Oh, the Places You'll Go! : 8580001038957: Seuss, Dr.: Books," accessed September 29, 2023, https://www.amazon.com/Oh-Places-Youll-Dr-Seuss/dp/0679805273/ref=sr_1_1?crid=263WI35OB CRSG&keywords=oh%2C+the+places+you%27ll+go&qid=1694859005&sprefix=oh%2C+the+p%2Caps%2C88&sr=8-1.
5. Expert Panel®, "Council Post: 13 Smart Ways To Add Value And Become A 'Network Benefit,'" Forbes, accessed October 9, 2023, https://www.forbes.com/sites/forbescoachescouncil/2021/03/31/13-smart-ways-to-add-value-and-b ecome-a-network-benefit/.
6. "Retaining Customers vs. New Customers: Methods and Benefits | Indeed.Com," accessed October 9, 2023, https://www.indeed.com/career-advice/career-development/retaining-customers-vs-new-customers.
7. Ann Howell, "How to Build Confidence at Work," *Harvard Business Review*, August 9, 2021, https://hbr.org/2021/08/how-to-build-confidence-at-work.
8. "Guide To Business Attire (With Examples) | Indeed.Com," accessed October 13, 2023, https://www.indeed.com/career-advice/starting-new-job/guide-to-business-attire.
9. "Apple Is the World's First $3 Trillion Company - WSJ," accessed November 27, 2023, https://www.wsj.com/articles/apple-three-trillion-dollar-company-e3ca1d4d?mod=Searchresults_po s1&page=1.
10. "How To Handle Rejection in Sales in 7 Steps (With Tips) | Indeed.Com," accessed November 27, 2023, https://www.indeed.com/career-advice/career-development/how-to-handle-rejection-in-sales.
11. "16 Types of Customer Needs (and How to Solve for Them)," March 24, 2023, https://blog.hubspot.com/service/customer-needs.

Epilogue & Final Super Hack 50 | 24 Years of Working with Inspirational Business Builders: 10 actionable insights
Self-Assessment Questions:

The following questions are meant to kick start internal conversations, introspection, and support for your entrepreneurial journey.

#1 **Adopt New Practices for Success:**

- How are you embracing change and staying updated with evolving practices?
- What new technologies or methodologies have you recently incorporated into your business approach?
- How can you refine your skills to prevent becoming obsolete?
- How actively are you seeking out changes in your industry or field?
- What steps are you taking to adapt to new trends, technologies, and market shifts?
- How do you handle unexpected disruptions or shifts in your business environment?
- What recent technological advancements have caught your attention?
- Have you explored and integrated any of these technologies into your business processes?
- How are you staying informed about emerging methodologies and best practices?
- What skills do you currently possess that are critical for your business success?
- How can you proactively enhance these skills to stay relevant?
- What learning opportunities (courses, workshops, mentorship) are you pursuing?

#2 **Establish Deep & Enduring Relationships.**

- What efforts are you making to cultivate meaningful connections with other professionals?
- How can you enhance the quality of your network beyond superficial interactions?
- Have you invested in others' success, and how has it benefited you personally and professionally?
- How are you intentionally building deeper relationships with other professionals?
- What steps are you taking to move beyond superficial interactions?
- Have you engaged in mentorship or collaborative projects with others?
- How diverse is your network regarding expertise, backgrounds, and industries?
- Are you nurturing relationships with people who inspire and challenge you?
- What value do you bring to your network, and how does it benefit both parties?
- How have you supported colleagues or fellow enterpreneurs in achieving their goals?
- What personal and professional rewards have you gained from investing in others?
- How can you continue to contribute to the success of those around you?

#3 **Carefully Craft Resources and Organizational Capabilities.**

- How are you balancing the pursuit of profits with sustainable practices?
- What steps have you taken to build lasting organizational capabilities?
- Are there specific resources (financial, human, technological) that need further development?
- How are you optimizing profitability without compromising long-term sustainability?
- What ethical considerations guide your resource allocation decisions?
- Have you explored environmentally friendly practices or social impact initiatives?
 What specific capabilities does your organization need to thrive?
- How are you developing and nurturing these capabilities over time?
- Are there gaps in your organizational structure or processes that require attention?
- What resources (financial, human, technological) are essential for your growth and development?
- What steps have you taken to secure and enhance these resources?
- How can you allocate resources and strategies to achieve your business objectives?

#4 *If* **Invest in Talent/Human Capital.**

- Have you made the most of available training resources to expand your skill set in the past quarter?
- Have you actively sought out mentorship opportunities to accelerate your professional growth and development?
- Can you pinpoint at least one new skill or area of knowledge you've gained through cross-functional projects or collaborations?
- How often do you engage in self-directed learning to stay ahead of industry trends and advancements?
- Have you contributed ideas or initiatives aimed at enhancing talent development within your team or organization?
- Do you actively seek feedback from peers and supervisors for improvement in your professional abilities?
- Have you taken on challenging assignments or projects outside your comfort zone?
- How effectively do you prioritize your time and resources to invest in both short-term skill development and long-term career growth?
- Do you actively participate in knowledge-sharing activities within your team or organization to foster a culture of continuous learning and growth?

#5 **Create Your Personal Brand.**

- Have you clearly defined your personal brand values?
- How effectively do you engage with your target audience to build trust and establish lasting connections?
- Can you identify specific strategies or initiatives you've implemented to enhance your personal brand authenticity?
- Do you actively seek feedback from customers or stakeholders to gauge the effectiveness of your branding efforts?
- Have you leveraged digital platforms and social media to expand your reach?
- Are you consistently delivering on your brand promises and commitments?
- How do you nurture relationships with strategic partners or collaborators to strengthen your market presence?
- Have you taken steps to differentiate yourself from competitors?
- Do you regularly evaluate and adjust your personal branding strategies based on market trends, feedback, and evolving consumer preferences?
- What actions do you take to ensure that every interaction contributes positively to your brand equity?

#6 Boost Productivity Through Technology.

- Have you sought out new technologies to increase productivity?
- Can you identify specific areas within your work processes where technology has helped you achieve efficiency?
- How frequently do you update your digital skills and knowledge?
- Have you leveraged automation tools or software to automate repetitive tasks?
- Are you proficient in using digital collaboration platforms to enhance teamwork and communication within your organization?
- Have you explored innovative technologies or solutions that could potentially revolutionize how you work or serve your customers?
- Do you actively seek feedback from colleagues or supervisors on how technology can be better utilized to improve productivity?
- Are you open to learning and adopting new technologies, even if they require some initial investment of time and effort?
- Have you identified any inefficiencies in your current workflow that could be addressed through the adoption of new technologies?
- How do you balance the use of technology with maintaining meaningful human interactions?

#7 Foster an Innovative Environment.

- Do you have an environment where innovative ideas are welcomed and encouraged?
- Can you identify specific instances where you or your team have embraced calculated risks to pursue innovative solutions?
- How do you foster a sense of belonging and community within your team to support a culture of innovation?
- Are you open to exploring unconventional approaches or perspectives?
- Have you participated in brainstorming sessions or idea generation exercises to stimulate creativity?
- Do you actively seek out opportunities to learn from failures and use them as stepping stones for the future?
- Have you implemented any processes or initiatives aimed at nurturing fresh ideas?
- How do you collaborate with colleagues from diverse backgrounds or departments to bring fresh perspectives to the table?
- Are you proactive in staying updated with industry trends and advancements?
- What measures do you take to ensure that innovative ideas are effectively communicated and implemented within your team or organization?

#8 __Emphasize Sustainable Leadership Practices.__

- Do you integrate environmental and social considerations into your decisions?
- Can you identify specific initiatives or practices you've implemented to promote sustainability?
- How do you ensure that ethical practices are upheld in your actions?
- Are you proactive in staying informed about emerging sustainability trends and best practices?
- Have you collaborated with stakeholders to develop and implement sustainability goals?
- Do you prioritize transparency and accountability in communicating your organization's sustainability efforts to stakeholders?
- Are you open to feedback and suggestions for improving sustainability practices within your leadership approach?
- Have you conducted assessments to measure the environmental and social impacts of your organization's activities?

9 __Advocate for Economic Opportunity & Prosperity for All.__

- Have you supported initiatives aimed at promoting economic opportunity and prosperity for all?
- Can you identify specific ways you have encouraged entrepreneurship?
- How do you foster an environment that encourages creativity and risk-taking, essential elements of entrepreneurship?
- Are you open to exploring diverse paths to entrepreneurship, recognizing that there's no one-size-fits-all approach?
- Have you provided mentorship or guidance to aspiring entrepreneurs?
- Do you advocate for policies or practices that remove barriers to entrepreneurship and promote inclusivity in business?
- Have you collaborated with community organizations or educational institutions to foster an entrepreneurial mindset among youth or underserved populations?
- How do you promote innovation and economic growth within your sphere of influence?
- Are you proactive in seeking out opportunities to support and invest in diverse entrepreneurial ventures?
- What steps do you take to empower individuals to pursue their aspirations?

#10 **Adopt an Adaptive Mindset.**

- How effectively do you challenge conventional norms in your approach to business?
- Can you identify specific instances where you've demonstrated adaptability in response to changing market conditions or disruptions?
- Do you actively seek out opportunities to learn from experiences?
- How do you cultivate emotional intelligence within yourself and your team?
- Are you transparent in your leadership approach, fostering open communication and trust within your organization?
- Do you prioritize the development of your team members' skills and character to ensure organizational longevity?
- Can you provide examples of how you've managed ambiguity and uncertainty to drive positive outcomes?
- Are you proactive in anticipating and responding to emerging trends or shifts in your industry?
- How do you foster a culture of adaptability and continuous improvement?
- What strategies do you employ to remain flexible and responsive to change while staying true to your organizational values and goals?

Epilogue & Final Super Hack 50
| 24 Years of Working with
Inspirational Business Builders: 10 actionable insights

Over the last twenty-four years, my interactions with numerous entrepreneurs have taught me valuable lessons that have helped them fast-track the growth of their innovative businesses. This process has been a natural evolution, fostering mutual inspiration and continuous adaptation and innovation.

A crucial part of my entrepreneurial journey has been cultivating advanced cognitive abilities (pattern recognition, intellectual curiosity, and life learning), which have been instrumental in navigating the intricate and ever-evolving business landscape.

Here, I present ten overarching insights for business-building success.

#1: **Adopt new practices for success.**

The business world is dynamic, and so are the practices that lead to success. What was <u>effective ten years ago</u>[1] might be outdated today. Experience underscores the significance of ongoing learning and adaptability.

It's crucial to embrace new technologies, methodologies, and best practices to stay competitive. We must continually refine our skills to prevent rapid obsolescence. Rapid experimentation, iteration, and fast pivots are hallmarks of success.

#2: **Establish deep & enduring relationships.**

A strong network has always been beneficial in business, and the digital era has made it simpler to connect with professionals globally. However, the quality of these connections is what truly counts.

Cultivating meaningful relationships[2] promotes collaboration, knowledge exchange, and access to valuable resources. Professionals are now prioritizing the development of deep and lasting connections, in-person and virtually, with readily available training and development resources. Invest deeply in others' success to reap personal and professional rewards.

#3: **Carefully craft resources and organizational capabilities.**

Businesses have realized that success isn't just about profits; it's also about building sustainable resources and organizational capabilities. A balanced focus on people, processes, profits, and the planet can coexist harmoniously.

Companies understand that they must invest in their people, technology, and infrastructure for long-term success. They are building a strong talent pool and optimizing processes. Importantly, for startups, resources should always trail opportunities, or the cash-efficient business model will be at risk.

#4: **Nurture talent/human capital.**

Investing in talent development[3] is now a fundamental part of modern business strategy. Companies recognize that their employees are their most valuable assets, whether through formal training programs, mentorship initiatives, or cross-functional projects.

Empowering employees to broaden their skills and take on new challenges benefits the individual and the company's overall capabilities and competitiveness. Make human capital more than a buzzword du jour. Invest smartly in organizational potential and capacity.

#5: **Create your brand.**

Establishing lasting connections with consumers and employees is vital in marketing and brand strategy. The digital age provides boundless opportunities for global reach, but quality interactions are paramount. Building trust through personal engagement with customers and strategic partnerships enhances brand loyalty, credibility, and market presence.

Personal brand authenticity[4] is your brand's core – it establishes how your messaging aligns with your values and actions and how people interact and connect emotionally to your brand. Your brand equity will incorporate your emotional connections with others, the follow-through on your commitments, and the actual experiences people have with you.

#6: **Boost productivity through technology.**

The advent of new technologies has transformed business operations.

Incorporating technology[5] into every aspect of the organization, from process streamlining to improved customer experiences, is not just an option but a necessity.

Companies that embrace these changes maintain their competitiveness and establish themselves as industry leaders. We all must be as

> Building a culture means focusing on people, valuing, and fostering a sense of belonging and community. It involves learning quickly from constructive failures and adeptly managing ongoing risks.

digitally savvy as GenZ-ers, productive, and efficient. This doesn't mean abandoning human interactions but enhancing our digital literacy to simplify and accelerate processes using technology.

Technology drives automation, productivity, and efficiency gains.

#7: **Foster an innovative environment.**

Innovation is the cornerstone of thriving businesses. Over the past two decades, the necessity for companies to foster an innovative culture to remain relevant has been underscored.

Encouraging employees to think outside the box, experiment with fresh ideas, and embrace calculated risks creates a setting where novel solutions can surface. Culture is often described as "how we do things around here."

#8: **Emphasize sustainable product leadership practices.**

Sustainability[6] has evolved from a buzzword to a business necessity. There's growing consciousness about business activities' environmental and social impacts. Companies prioritizing sustainable practices contribute to a healthier planet and enhance their brand reputation.

Those who exemplify responsible environmental, social & governance (ESG) approaches, uphold ethical practices, and incorporate this thinking into their leadership, and product decisions will reap benefits.

#9: **Advocate for economic opportunity & prosperity for all.**

Entrepreneurship democratizes the field,[7] granting every driven and interested individual the freedom to control their destiny and carve their unique path. The most inspiring lesson I've gleaned from all the entrepreneurs I've worked with is that there's no single correct way, time, or business concept to be entrepreneurial. The spark comes from "just doing it."

#10: **Adopt an adaptive mindset.**

The most crucial business lesson from the past two decades is thinking differently. Disruption is the new status quo, and adaptability is the survival key. Businesses that have prospered are those willing to challenge conventional norms, embrace innovation, and take calculated risks.

Adaptiveness is a fundamental characteristic of successful business-builders. Adaptive leadership[8] embodies important traits – emotional intelligence, organizational transparency, development, and character. Together, these traits provide the essential tools for organizational longevity.

Final Thoughts

My over two decades of business insights have underscored the importance of enhancing higher-order thinking skills and learning from digging deep into other's generous spirits and the myriad of experiences that have shaped and honed your leadership voice. These principles will continue to shape the future of business, guiding us toward sustained growth and success in an ever-evolving world.

Flexibility, managing ambiguity, and responding situationally to changing business conditions are the defining traits of an effective business builder.

End Notes for Epilogue & Final Super Hack 50

1. Clare Moore, "Council Post: Embracing The One Constant In Business: Change," Forbes, accessed April 26, 2024, https://www.forbes.com/sites/forbesbusinesscouncil/2021/03/30/embracing-the-one-constant-in-business-change/.
2. Bart Foster, "4 Strategies for Building Deep Business Relationships," Entrepreneur, January 4, 2023, https://www.entrepreneur.com/living/4-strategies-for-building-deep-business-relationships/441969.
3. Jeffrey M. Cohn, Rakesh Khurana, and Laura Reeves, "Growing Talent as If Your Business Depended on It," *Harvard Business Review*, October 1, 2005, https://hbr.org/2005/10/growing-talent-as-if-your-business-depended-on-it.
4. Michael Georgiou, "Council Post: How And Why To Build Brand Authenticity," Forbes, accessed April 26, 2024, https://www.forbes.com/sites/forbescommunicationscouncil/2021/03/15/how-and-why-to-build-bran d-authenticity/.
5. Pavel Stepanov, "Council Post: A Guide To Implementing New Technologies Effectively In The Workplace," Forbes, accessed April 26, 2024, https://www.forbes.com/sites/forbesbusinesscouncil/2023/07/26/a-guide-to-implementing-new-technologies-effectively-in-the-workplace/.
6. "What Is Sustainability in Business? | IBM," March 20, 2024, https://www.ibm.com/topics/business-sustainability.
7. Kartik Jobanputra, "Council Post: Entrepreneurship: The Engine Of Growth Driving Our Economy," Forbes, accessed April 26, 2024, https://www.forbes.com/sites/forbesbusinesscouncil/2023/07/31/entrepreneurship-the-engine-of-gro wth-driving-our-economy/.
8. "Adaptive Leadership," Corporate Finance Institute, accessed April 26, 2024, https://corporatefinanceinstitute.com/resources/management/adaptive-leadership/.

50 Habits & Mind Shifts to Make You Better

Within this book, you'll find callout boxes that emphasize essential behavioral habit changes and mindset shifts. These adjustments and "tweaks" can lead to personal and professional growth. **Consider selecting 3-5 of these shifts each year** and commit to mastering them. By doing so, you'll fully realize your potential and become an improved version of yourself and proactively improve your "absorptive capacity".

1. Leadership & Organizational Culture

💡 Make sure you set aside time each day to do something that brings you joy, such as exercising, reading a book, or spending time with loved ones. These choices will help you avoid living with regret.

💡 To make a shift in your company culture, you need to realize it is an ongoing process that requires dedication, commitment, and continuous evaluation. What steps could you take?

💡 Take a moment to reconnect with your original inspiration. Reflect on what ignited your entrepreneurial journey, the problems you aimed to solve, or the impact you wanted to make. Revisit your core purpose. Reaffirm your "why."[8]

💡 Create a strategic roadmap that outlines your goals, timelines, and actionable steps. Develop processes and systems to streamline operations, delegate responsibilities, and foster collaboration among your team members.

💡 Highlight your organization's unique selling points and leverage them to create a distinct identity in the minds of consumers.

💡 Attention to detail is a hallmark of uber-successful companies that achieve consistent, high-impact results. Companies that reach that hallmark have leaders who delegate, inspire, and collaborate with their team members.

💡 By exploring different possibilities and outcomes, they can anticipate challenges and seize opportunities others might miss. This habit enables them to innovate and remain agile in an ever-changing business landscape.

💡 Consistency in branding builds trust. Customers notice when you consistently adhere to your stated vision and values – and they feel a sense of security interacting with you.

💡 One of the best pieces of advice I have received is to "live your life in the windshield, not in the rearview mirror." Thinking back, it is probably a much healthier place to be.

2. Innovation & Entrepreneurship

💡 Encourage employees to hone and build their skills while learning to connect the dots.

💡 Step out of your comfort zone. Pursue new career paths. Explore different passions.

💡 By recognizing the limitations of technology and embracing the power of human connection, businesses can build stronger relationships with their customers. High tech can undoubtedly enable speedy interactions, but high touch will still win.

💡 Whether through local meetups, online communities, or international conferences, intentional networking and communication enable entrepreneurs to tap into a wealth of knowledge, gather diverse perspectives, and collaborate on projects that transcend boundaries.

💡 Shifting employees into different roles allows you to tap into their diverse skill sets and knowledge. You can help your workforce acquire new competencies and adapt to new responsibilities by providing training and development programs.

💡 In the dynamic business world, trying new things and learning from failure is not just a choice but also a necessity. While we often associate failure with negative connotations, it can be a powerful catalyst for growth and success.

💡 Seek support from mentors, peers, or business communities to gain new perspectives and guidance. You can transform setbacks into stepping stones toward success by redirecting negative emotions into positive action.

💡 All competitive advantages erode over time, so looking for new opportunities to shift and pursue unique advantages is critical.

💡 Entrepreneurs should strive to create an experience beyond the product, making customers feel valued and providing an inviting and welcoming atmosphere that encourages repeat visits.

💡 Involving the user early in development is a great way to uncover valuable insights. Prototyping and iterative testing allow for rapid refinement, ensuring your innovation meets expectations.

💡 Embrace the journey of trial and error and pivots, as it may lead to unexpected and superior solutions.

💡 Instead of blaming external factors, successful entrepreneurs see problems as opportunities for growth and innovation. They control their destiny by owning the problem and empowering themselves to create impactful solutions.

💡 By diversifying approaches and testing new ideas, you create an atmosphere where innovation thrives. Encouraging cross-functional collaboration supports diverse ideas, which can lead to groundbreaking solutions.

3. Marketing & Branding

💡 For all the attention paid to celebrity endorsements, recent surveys show "brand mascots (like Aflac Duck, Flo from Progressive, and Pillsbury Doughboy) are more effective than celebrities."

💡 Remember to keep the experience personal. Sometimes, we over-automate experiences at the expense of high-touch activities. High-touch activities can often reinforce critical components of the brand promise.

💡 Establish legitimacy by obtaining the licenses, permits, and certifications relevant to your industry. These credentials demonstrate your compliance with regulations and signify your commitment to quality, excellence and professionalism.

💡 Conduct thorough market research[12] to uncover industry gaps, trends, and opportunities. Define your niche based on demographics, psychographics, and behavioral patterns.

4. Personal & Business Development

💡 Adding learning journeys or mandatory fun days can also get your team out of the office, boost your knowledge, foster new connections, and gain broader insights.

💡 By accumulating experience, you can develop a mental toolkit to face future challenges. That's how you can learn to think creatively, pivot quickly, and make sound decisions amidst enormous uncertainty.

💡 Crowdfunding has altered the startup landscape by offering a unique way to secure funding, validate ideas, and build a community. By embracing this modern approach, you can tap into the power of the crowd, fostering a culture of innovation that benefits both creators and backers alike.

💡 You can create a lasting impression by engaging their emotions and vividly portraying your mission. Remember, a compelling story can help investors see the potential beyond the figures and foster a genuine interest in your venture.

💡 Evaluating your team critically is crucial in determining whether you are genuinely investment-worthy. Assess each team member's relevant experience and expertise, considering how their skills align with the venture's needs.

💡 When evaluating a funding round, investors should consider your startup's growth trajectory, market potential, competitive landscape, inherent risks, and likelihood of achieving financial projections. What things can you do to derisk a key assumption in your business?

💡 Positivity is contagious, so embracing new opportunities can create a ripple effect of positivity that will benefit others in their pursuits.

💡 Stay in touch through emails, phone calls, or social media platforms – sending a news article relevant to their work can go a long way. Engage in networking events, conferences, and industry gatherings to expand your circle and build new connections.

💡 Aim to create a <u>pricing strategy</u>[41] that reflects your value while ensuring your venture's sustainability and profitability. You can price your product multiple ways, so determine which works best based on your market and industry.

💡 Conduct thorough research and consider the potential consequences before taking a public stance on sensitive issues. Striking a balance between authenticity and avoiding unnecessary controversy is vital to maintaining a positive brand image.

💡 To tackle demand issues, businesses should focus on smart growth - steady, controlled growth where quality, efficiency, and support systems are conducive to achieving the growth goals.

💡 Leveraging digital marketing tools and social media platforms can significantly boost your brand's visibility and attract a wider audience. Adopting an <u>omnichannel approach</u> [51] ensures a seamless customer experience, attracting new customers while fostering loyalty.

💡 Be open to feedback when seeking advice, even if it challenges your initial beliefs. Constructive criticism can help you identify weaknesses in your business idea and explore alternative approaches.

💡 Setting practical goals is a delicate balance between your ambition and reality. However, by making them realistic, breaking down big dreams into small steps, and knowing your limits, you can pave the way for consistent growth without the risk of burnout.

💡 Learning to say "no" strategically can be a powerful tool. Prioritize meetings that align with your current objectives and directly impact your business. Politely decline invitations to gatherings that don't contribute significantly to your goals or can be addressed through other means of communication.

💡 Instead of succumbing to imposter syndrome, seek mentors and educational resources and make progress, even small ones, toward your goals. Those actions can provide a powerful antidote to the poison of imposter syndrome.

💡 By intertwining your mission with your business, you find joy, excitement, and fulfillment in your work and become a more authentic advocate for your cause and advancing your vision.

💡 You can't perpetually pivot forever, but you can pivot when necessary. Ultimately, I'm saying this: it isn't about the failure, but how you respond and recover from it.

💡 Ask yourself and your team, "Are we delighted with what we're doing?" (are we passionately and highly engaged in what we are doing?)

5. <u>Networking & Relationship Building</u>

💡 Like you would in Vegas, place your bets. Find what gives you joy and inspiration -- whether professional development, industry association participation, learning journeys, reading, attending trade shows, or taking online classes.

💡 By consistently delivering value through your media content, you attract like-minded individuals and potential business partners who resonate with your message and will likely engage and collaborate with you.

💡 One way to exhibit confidence is through body language. Stand tall, make eye contact, and offer a firm handshake when appropriate. Additionally, speak clearly and confidently, expressing your thoughts and ideas without hesitation.

💡 Focusing on smaller milestones allows you to step back down the road and see how these small steps culminate in success.

6. Epilogue

Building a culture means focusing on people, valuing and fostering a sense of belonging and community. It involves learning quickly from constructive failures and adeptly managing ongoing risks.

GREATER GATOR FUND

Join us in providing higher quality, proven business-building services to support next generation entrepreneurs by providing a tax-deductible donation at the QR code below:

ABOUT THE BOOK

50 Super E-Hacks serves as a guide, motivating entrepreneurs to navigate the intricate landscape of business development. Drawing from extensive experience and distilled wisdom, it offers nuanced strategies to empower entrepreneurs at every stage of their journey. Born from my original work, *Entrepreneurial Hacks | Practical Insights for Business Builders*, these insights provide unique perspectives. I encourage you to embrace introspection and deliberate engagement with self-assessment inquiries, and consider areas for improvement and innovation wherever possible. Each section is rich with actionable advice and real-world illustrations, facilitating seamless integration into daily operations. Whether launching a startup or steering an established enterprise, use these resources to better yourself, your business, and at the forefront...your community. **Aspire higher in everything you do and dream**. Mediocrity is miserable.

ABOUT THE AUTHOR

Karl R LaPan is a business professional with over 38 years of experience in consumer, industrial, technology, health care services and financial companies. Currently, he is the Director of UF Innovate|Accelerate leading one of the largest university owned and operated super hubs and entrepreneurial support organizations in the United States.

From 2000, he has served as President & CEO of the Northeast Indiana Innovation Center/Park (The NIIC), an entrepreneurial community dedicated to accelerating the development of entrepreneurs, business builders and innovative companies.

Over the past twenty-four years, he has worked with thousands of entrepreneurs, community leaders, educators, thought leaders, and business builders to advance proven business techniques and models to build and grow successful businesses and viable and valuable ventures.

Mr. LaPan is a student of business and entrepreneurship. He is an in-demand, thought leader and speaker on customer service, loyalty, creativity and innovation, marketing and management strategy, entrepreneurial growth, business and strategic planning and leadership. He has been the recipient of several local and regional awards and has authored and co-authored numerous books, articles, and blogs on business innovation, creativity and entrepreneurship. He also teaches several entrepreneurial courses at the undergrad and graduate level.